Eternal Security For True Believers

The Rabin Assassination—Predicted

An Excerpt from The End of History —
Messiah Conspiracy Volume II — Essays

Philip N. Moore
Researcher for Hal Lindsey

The Conspiracy, Incorporated
Atlanta, GA
1997

Published by The Conspiracy, Incorporated
P. O. Box 12227, Atlanta, GA, USA 30355
Toll Free: 1-800-RAMS HEAD (1-800-726-7432)
E-Mail: theconinc@aol.com
Fax: 404-816-9994

Printed in the United States of America

Scripture taken from the NEW AMERICAN STANDARD BIBLE (R), Harper Study Edition, © Copyright The Lockman Foundation 1960, 1962, 1963, 1968, 1971, 1972, 1973, 1975, 1977. Used by permission. Quotations of the Hebrew Bible taken from the BIBLIA HEBRAICA STUTTGARTENSIA, © Copyright 1966, 1977, 1983, German Bible Society. Used by permission. The Hebraica and Symbol Greek Mono fonts used to print this work is available from Linguist's Software, Inc., PO Box 580, Edmonds, WA, USA 98020-0580. Tel. (206) 775-1130.

Moore, Philip N., 1957-
        The End of History—Messiah Conspiracy Volume II—Essays—
        Exerpt—Eternal Security for True Believers, with appendices excerpted from Vol. I, Vol. II, and Nightmare of the Apocalypse, by Philip N. Moore.

ISBN 1-57915-999-0
        1. Religion—Prophecy
        2. History—Biblical
        3. Christianity—Judaism
Library of Congress Catalog Card Number: 97-66134

In memory of my grandfather, George Moore, Sr.*, and my loving father, Nicholas George Moore, without whose support the research and writing of this book would not have been possible. Also, to my mother Marie and my brother Paul, who have been so understanding over the course of my writing. And finally, to the Messiah Jesus, who is my best friend, for comfort and guidance.

---

*Lower right inset.

"A Star of Bethelehem created by planetary conjunction neatly dovetails with...beliefs of the time. The Jupiter-Saturn conjunction...would have occurred in Pisces, a constellation that has been considered the "house of the Hebrew"...Historical inferences also suggest that Jupiter was associated with Yahweh, the God of Israel, and Saturn with the Messiah....British astronomer David Hughes writes: 'We have here ample justification for concluding that the Jupiter-Saturn conjunction in Pisces had a strong, clear...message. To Babylonians and Jews alike, it heralded the coming of the Messiah, a man of righteousness who would save the world.'"[1]   David Stamps

If you desire to see the fascinating beauty of this constellation/con-junction recorded in Matthew 2:16, it is now possible to do so. Thanks to modern science, you can go back in time, so to speak, by visiting the planetarium. Above is a photograph of an astral reproduction of the 2000-year-old constellation of Pisces with the three planets, Mars, Saturn and Jupiter. This photograph was taken at the Fernbank Science Center planetarium in Atlanta, Georgia. (See our Volume I, Chapter 5, for documentary details on the prophecy of the Star of Bethlehem.)

---

[1]David Stamps, "What Was the Star of Bethlehem?" *National Wildlife*, Dec.-Jan. 1988, pp. 18-19, © used by permission. Photo by Philip Moore.

TABLE OF CONTENTS

The Messiah rose from the dead, lives today, and will return soon!
Meanwhile, all those who put their faith in Him are eternally secure.

"I am a Jew, but I am enthralled by the luminous figure of the Nazarene....No one can read the Gospels without feeling the actual presence of Jesus. His personality pulsates in every word. No myth is filled with such life." [1]   Albert Einstein, October 26, 1929

---

[1]Arthur W. Kac, *The Messiahship of Jesus,* Grand Rapids, MI: Baker Bookhouse © 1980, p. 36, used by permission. Kac's source was *The Saturday Evening Post*, Oct. 26, 1929.

"But if we walk in the light, as he is in the light, we have fellowship one with another, and the blood of Jesus Christ, his Son, cleanseth us from all sin. If we say that we have no sin, we are deceiving ourselves, and the truth is not in us....If we confess our sins, He is faithful and just to forgive us *our* sins, and to cleanse us from all unrighteousness. If we say that we have not sinned, we make him a liar, and his word is not in us."   I John 1:7-10; KJV[1]

"These things I have written to you who believe in the name of the Son of God, in order that you may know that you have eternal life."   I John 5:13 NASB

"...and not through the blood of goats and calves, but through His own blood, He entered the holy place once for all, having obtained eternal redemption."
Hebrews 9:12 NASB

"All that the Father gives Me will come to Me, and the one who comes to Me I will certainly not cast out. For I have come down from heaven, not to do My own will, but the will of Him who sent Me. And this is the will of Him who sent Me, that of all that He has given Me I lose nothing, but raise it up on the last day."
John 6:37-40 NASB

ETERNAL SECURITY
FOR TRUE BELIEVERS

I have heard some very well-meaning and profoundly convicted preachers and Christians sarcastically say, "Let's not think that because someone says a little prayer to Jesus, that secures his salvation. That's not in the Bible anywhere. That's a Baptist idea, etc." and on and on. Well, we, as Bible believers, must take exception to all of these false insinuations, usually made by charismatic brothers who are not up on their Bible study.

GOD'S ETERNAL SALVATION PRAYER
EXISTS IN OUR BIBLE, NO MATTER HOW MANY
DAMNATION PREACHERS WISH IT DID NOT !

Paul, who was not one of these "Baptists," wrote: "That if thou shalt confess with thy mouth the Lord Jesus, and shalt believe in thine heart that God hath raised him from the dead, thou shalt be **saved**" (Rom. 10:9 KJV). Therefore, that "little prayer" which certain legalistic preachers may criticize, called the sinners' prayer, contains the above sentiment and admits that we need the atoning blood of Jesus and, of course, expresses the belief that He was raised from the dead and that He is ready to return and redeem the world and its inhabitants

---

[1]*The New Scofield Reference Bible.*

one day (Rom. 8:23; 11:15).[2] Thus, we can assure you with complete certainty that this salvation promise **is in the Bible** and means exactly what it says.   Saved is a word, which means **saved** forever, not temporarily preserved.

Hal Lindsey, the famous Christian author, once said: "Salvation isn't like a game of horseshoes, you can't get close, you're either saved or you're not." So once saved, you're not to be lost.

I have often heard the clichés from well-meaning charismatic preachers. "I get them saved, but I can't keep them saved." Nothing could be more false than this statement. Once saved means always saved, because saved means exactly what it says—saved! The word does not imply "preserved for a time" until we go too far—who is to say what is too far, none of us are perfect. For those of us who have accepted Jesus as our savior and fall short of God's will from time to time, the Bible says: "If we are faithless, He remains faithful; for He cannot deny Himself" (II Tim. 2:13 NASB).

In the first book of the Hebrew Bible, we are introduced to the fall—the fall involved the serpent who was indwelt by Satan himself. The venom he injected into the human race, which brought about the fall and incurred our present fallen sin nature, can only be counteracted by antivenin. Jesus' blood is the antivenin! Once you receive antivenin in the hospital, your life is saved from destruction from that venom. At a later date the venom doesn't reactivate, it works once for all. So it is with Jesus. If we receive His antivenim, the condition of the sin nature is dealt with "once for all" as Hebrews 9:12 tells us.

YOU MIGHT LOSE YOUR REWARDS, BUT
YOU WILL NEVER LOSE YOUR SALVATION

My wholehearted support of the biblical doctrine of eternal security is directed against those who think God should squash and smash a believer who falls back into the ways of the world for a while. God will by no means forsake a brother who becomes rebellious because someone has laid a guilt trip on him.

There is a consequence to remaining out of fellowship with the Lord if it is kept up strenuously for a prolonged period of time. But it is not the loss of Jesus' perfect forever salvation. The Bible says if someone refuses to repent, he may be called home sooner than

---

[2]"And not only this, but also we ourselves, having the first fruits of the Spirit, even we ourselves groan within ourselves, waiting eagerly for *our* adoption as sons, the redemption of our body....For if their [the Jews] rejection [of the Messiah] be the reconciliation of the world, what will *their* acceptance be but life from the dead [resurrection, i.e., the millennial kingdom]?" (Romans 8:23; 11:15 NASB [ ] mine).

planned. In other words, he will die before his time because God has realized he is no more earthly good to the kingdom. He may lose certain rewards he gained beforehand (I Cor. 3:14-15), but he will not lose Jesus' perfect salvation. Jesus does not take back what he genuinely gave.

THE MOST HEINOUS SIN MENTIONED IN
THE NEW TESTAMENT DID NOT MERIT HELL
FOR AN OUT OF FELLOWSHIP BELIEVER!

Read the story in I Corinthians 5:1-5. For example, one of the most horrible sins we can imagine is told of whereby a son and his father's wife (his stepmother), are involved in adultery. Paul never says that the son has lost his salvation, as some contemporary hellfire and damnation preachers would like to believe. Paul says, "Let's deliver his flesh over to Satan, so that his spirit might be **saved**."

Note that, even in this terrible state, Paul never says he's going to be in Hell. To the contrary, in the second letter to the Corinthians, Paul tells the church to receive this person back into fellowship after he repented (II Cor. 2:6-11). Paul only wanted him out of the congregation while he was involved in this most heinous sin.

SOME SAY ETERNAL SECURITY IS
"THE MOST DANGEROUS DOCTRINE"
BUT IT IS ONLY DANGEROUS TO SATAN

Notwithstanding, we should realize that God is much more merciful than we are. We have no right to tell others that Jesus' atonement may not be sufficient for their sins, when **He** died on their behalf. Do not forget, you too, brother or preacher, may one day fall into the same trap and the shoe may be on the other foot! Reverend Jimmy Swaggart was one who always taught against eternal security, claiming it as the "most dangerous doctrine." If anyone needed God's mercy, of course, we all know this person did. I have not heard him teach against eternal security since his hypocrisy was exposed.[3]

Paul teaches in I Corinthians 6:9-10 that: "Or do you not know that the unrighteous shall not inherit the kingdom of God? Do not be

---

[3]On his second fall, when he was caught in the car with a prostitute, he refused to apologize to his congregation, very unlike his first episode when he publicly repented and asked humble forgiveness from his wife, family and all. To our knowledge, he has yet to issued a statement of apology or repentance or even sorrow to his family or anyone else. God promised the sure mercies of David to those who humbly come before Him (Ps. 51), but we have to be willing to come before God and lose our pride before His great honor.

deceived;   neither fornicators, nor idolaters, nor adulterers, nor effeminate, nor homosexuals, nor thieves, nor *the* covetous, nor drunkards, nor revilers, nor swindlers, shall inherit the kingdom of God" (NASB).

Are you worried? Did you wonder if you might have had a drink too many or yelled too harshly at your wife, mom, brother or sister? Don't be because God is able to forgive even you and even me. Remember the Bible says that worry is also a sin! Don't worry, just confess—confess constantly and secretly to Jesus and you will not be guilty—you will not even feel guilt if you accept the fact that He forgives you unconditionally. He took your guilt. If you worry or doubt that you are forgiven, it is like telling Him He did not die for your guilt.

IF YOU STUMBLE INTO SIN, AS A *BELIEVER,* DO NOT LOSE ALL HOPE, BECAUSE JESUS HAS PAID FOR *ALL!*

The above verses needlessly frighten many who believe in Jesus as Savior. Believers who have been washed in the blood, who are eternally saved and redeemed, have no doubt committed some of these sins at different times[4] in their lives, though not habitually. The Bible says Jesus died to pay for the above (I John 1:9; I Peter 2:24). Peter says, "By his wounds you were healed." Past tense. These verses are not meant to condemn those who have been born-again, and, at times, fall into one of these sins; rather, the passage describes sins that condemn all of unredeemed humanity to Hell![5]

These scriptures refer to those who have no forgiveness, because they have rejected or have not accepted the one who paid the penalty for all sins! Paul says in Colossians 1:13-14; 2:13,[6] that Jesus took all [not 99%] of our sins out of the way by way of the cross. These include the sins He died for from the *foundation* of the world, which at that time included the last sin we would do—even those that are future.

---

[4]After you asked Jesus into your heart, have you ever gotten drunk at a party or reviled someone for something you were upset about? Have you ever gotten the better end of a deal by swindling someone? Have you ever wanted something which belonged to someone else? If you did, you were coveting—*after* you were a believer. Perhaps you have not, but many have! And the blood of Jesus will protect them from His judgment as He promised. We hold onto the love and blood of Jesus, never to let go, no matter who tries to make us!

[5]See our *Volume I,* Chapter 1, where we cover the fall and original sin from a biblical and Jewish perspective.

[6]"For He delivered us from the domain of darkness, and transferred us to the kingdom of His beloved Son, in whom we have redemption, the forgiveness of sins....And when you were dead in your transgressions and the uncircumcision of your flesh, He made you alive together with Him, having forgiven us **all** our transgressions...." (NASB).

The verses in question in I Corinthians 6 should concern those who *scoff* at Jesus' atonement for their sins. These verses pose no threat to those whose very sins Jesus has paid for, as He takes up residence in their hearts.

These individuals who have received Jesus are the eternally secure, who no matter how many times they fall or even willingly jump into these things, will never be condemned, because of Jesus' promise. "He who believes in Him [our Savior, Jesus] is not judged; he who does not believe has been judged already...." (John 3:18 NASB).

Jesus clarifies this with his very own words in the strongest possible way: "Verily, verily, I say unto you, He that heareth my word, and believeth on him that sent me, hath everlasting life, and shall not come into condemnation; but is passed from death unto life" (John 5:24 KJV).

IF YOU PERSIST IN SERIOUS SIN, YOU WILL NOT LOSE YOUR ETERNAL SALVATION- YOU'LL LOSE YOUR EARTHLY LIFE!

If a believer in Jesus persists in defying his creator, he will die a premature death! Even though God may severely discipline him in this life, he will not be abandoned to Hell; rather Jesus' salvation is still valid even for him. However, he will lose rewards (I Cor. 3:14-15)[7] he would have had a chance to receive, through the works done for the Lord in faith, which he would have not been able to do because he was "called home" (Eph. 5:15-16).[8] We know that if he refuses to cease activities which involve habitual and prolonged sins, he will die before his time, however, he will be with the Lord. For John affirms to us that there is a sin unto death (I John 5:16).

THE BACKSLIDER WHO NEVER COMES BACK, WAS *NEVER* THERE—NO ONE CAN TAKE THE TRUE BELIEVER OUT OF GOD'S HAND!

Jesus is called the "source of **eternal** salvation" (Heb. 5:9 NASB). We are reminded in the Bible that despite our sins and

---

[7]"If any man's work abide which he hath built thereupon, he shall receive a reward. If any man's work shall be burned, he shall suffer loss: but he himself shall be saved; yet so as by fire" (KJV).

[8]This passage refers to purchasing something out of eternity for oneself, a reward. This is what is meant by redeeming the times. Only the believer has the opportunity to do this as he tells others and is an example to others, while his limited years pass he can wisely use his time: "See then that ye walk circumspectly, not as fools, but as wise, Redeeming the time, because the days are evil" (Eph. 5:15-16 KJV).

faithlessness: "If we are faithless, He remains faithful; for He cannot deny Himself" (II Tim. 2:6 NASB). You may be right when you ask, "What about backsliders who never come back?"

In many cases, these individuals were never true believers! Only God knows the person's heart and his true decision! The apostle John tells us: "They went out from us, but they were not *really* of us; for if they had been of us, they would have remained with us; but *they went out*, in order that it might be shown that they all are not of us" (I John 2:19 NASB).

Apostates are not, and **never** were, born-again! Jesus tells us in John's Gospel: "My sheep hear My voice, and I know them, and they follow Me; and I give **eternal** [not temporary] life to them, and they shall **never** perish; and **no one** shall snatch them out of **My hand**. My Father, who has given *them* to Me, is greater than all; and no one is able to snatch *them* out of the Father's hand. I and the Father are one' " (John 10:27-30 NASB, [ ] and bold mine).

IF YOU ARE SINNING LESS BECAUSE
YOU ARE AFRAID YOU ARE GOING TO HELL,
YOU ARE DOING IT FOR THE WRONG REASON

The motive to sin less lies in our great thankfulness for what the Messiah has done for us! The false idea that if we do not walk the chalk line, we might "go to Hell" is a legalistic concept, not a biblical one! The scriptures make this clear when they say: "And do not grieve the Holy Spirit of God, by whom you were sealed for the day of redemption" (Eph. 4:30 NASB).

THE *FAITHFUL* OF ISRAEL WILL BE ETERNALLY
WITH US BECAUSE OF THEIR FAITH IN GOD'S
PROVISIONS AND THE MESSIAH

In the Old Testament we are taught: "Israel has been saved by the LORD with an everlasting salvation; You will not be put to shame or humiliated To all eternity....Incline your ear and come to Me. Listen, that you may live; And I will make an everlasting covenant with you, *According to* the faithful mercies shown to David" (Isa. 45:17; 55:3 NASB).

Remember what David did with Bath-sheba and her husband? He committed murder and adultery, yet the Bible teaches us he was shown faithful mercies (Psalm 51)!

Ezekiel emphasizes, in God's very words: "And I will make a covenant of peace with them; it will be an everlasting covenant with them. And I will place them and multiply them, and will set My sanctuary in their midst forever. My dwelling place also will be with them; and I will be their God, and they will be My people. And the nations will know that I am the LORD who sanctifies Israel, when My sanctuary is in their midst forever" (Ezek. 37:26-28 NASB).

The above speaks of a time when the Messiah Jesus will return to earth, resurrect the dead who have believed in his atonement and reign in the Messianic kingdom so often spoken of throughout our Bible! (See my chapters 29-30 in *The End of History—Messiah Conspiracy Volume I* for extensive details on these subjects.)

WHAT OF THAT SCARY VERSE IN MATTHEW ABOUT "ENDURING UNTIL THE END"?

Zola Levitt, a precious Jewish Christian, and author of over forty books on the Bible, has insightfully noted of Jesus' words: "But he that shall endure unto the end, the same shall be saved" (Matt. 24:13 KJV). "Some have utilized this remark to indicate that a certain level of purity must be maintained on the part of the saints in order to preserve their own salvation throughout the times of these evil signs. But again if we'll apply the rule of the King of the Jews instructing his subjects, we will see that the verse applies appropriately to unredeemed Israel. Those Jews who endure entirely until the return of the Lord— who simply survive in whatever spiritual condition—will be those who 'look upon Him whom they have pierced' (Zech. 12:10), and 'mourn for Him as for an only son' (Zech. 12:10). The net result of this atonement on the part of surviving Israel is found in Paul's exaltation in Romans 11:26: 'And so all Israel shall be saved: as it is written, There shall come out of Zion the Deliverer, and shall turn away ungodliness from Jacob.' "[9]

It is clear from the context of these words that our Lord is addressing a dispensation within the great tribulation, which the 24th chapter of Matthew speaks of. Read the chapter again and you'll see that it in no way refers to blood bought believers "enduring in their purity or behavior or else" as some would have us believe!

CAN HE WHO *OVERCOMES*, REALLY OVERCOME? WHAT DOES "OVERCOME" TRULY MEAN ANYWAY?

Revelation 2:7 says: "He who has an ear, let him hear what the Spirit says to the churches. To him who overcomes, I will grant to eat of the tree of life, which is in the Paradise of God" (NASB). Revelation 2:17 says: "He who has an ear, let him hear what the Spirit says to the churches. To him who **overcomes**, to him I will give *some* of the hidden manna, and I will give him a white stone, and a new name written on the stone which no one knows but he who receives it" (NASB, bold mine).

---

[9]Zola Levitt, *The Signs of the End*. Dallas: Zola Levitt Ministries, © 1978, pp. 5-6, used by permission (see page 10 ibid. to properly understand the parable of the virgins).

Revelation 21:7 says: "He who **overcomes** shall inherit these things, and I will be his God and he will be My son" (NASB, bold mine). Some are alarmed at this, thinking that we've got to *overcome* all of our shortcomings and mistakes to achieve a state which is one step short of perfection. However, the apostle John clarifies what overcome means. **John tells us** that overcome means to "simply believe in Jesus and his forgiveness" when he writes: "And who is the **one who overcomes** the world, but he who **believes** that Jesus is the Son of God?" (I John 5:5 NASB).

The one who *overcomes* is identified in I John as a person who simply accepts Jesus as Messiah. Jesus verifies this with his very own words: "...'This is the work of God, that ye believe on him whom he hath sent' " (John 6:29 KJV). It is not some superior spiritual goody goody, who seems to get everything right all of the time, as some would have us believe. In Matthew 7:21-23, Jesus affirms many of those who did things in His name[10] will not be in the Kingdom, but those who do the will of His father will be. The will of the father is for us to believe and accept Jesus. We are saved by God's work, as we have shown, and not by our own works or good deeds. The New Testament tells us in Ephesians: "For by grace you have been saved through faith; and that not of yourselves, *it is* the **gift** of God; not as a result of works, that no one should boast" (Eph. 2:8-9 NASB).[11]

REASONS FOR BELIEVING IN ETERNAL SECURITY, AND WHY THERE ARE SOME WHO DON'T WANT YOU TO KNOW WHY!

The main reason you should realize and appreciate the importance of eternal security is that this treasured biblical truth will

---

[10] No doubt there are phony preachers using His name for financial gain when they do not even believe He ever existed. On that *day* (of judgement) it's too late to call Jesus Lord.

[11] Some legalistic and ecumenical officials may argue, "But James says faith without works is dead." Here we must answer with the truth, *that works,* are the product of true faith. If there is no evidence of faithful and good works, then the faith probably is not genuine. In other words, if you are not giving out Bibles and books, attempting to share your faith with your friends so that they will be in the kingdom with you, you probably do not believe it yourself. Thus, your faith is faulty. The verse does not mean, as some try to teach, that you must help God to save you by adding your own good works to the work of Jesus' sacrifice for us. That would be saying Jesus' death is not enough! Remember, the thief on the cross, who Jesus said would be in paradise with Him, did not a single good work, nor was he baptized. Some teach that you must be baptized along with faith to be assured of Jesus' kingdom. The Bible says all we must do is believe. To say anything contradicting these words of Jesus is blasphemy and will be dealt with by Him on judgment day. The Bible says that many false prophets will go out into the world. I would not trade anything in the world to be in their shoes on judgment day, would you?

give you rock solid confidence, so you can rest, secure in your faith, destiny and sharing of Jesus with others. The reasons many people put off or reject receiving Jesus as Savior is because they feel they are not "ready yet" and may lose their salvation after getting it, due to their lack of willingness to strive toward *perfection*.

There are people who called themselves theologians denying the truth of eternal security, teaching we must strive toward an impossible "holy perfection," or else. However, Jesus once said: "For my yoke *is* easy, and my burden is light" (Matt. 11:30 KJV). Peter has written unto us: "Casting all your care upon him; for he careth for you" (I Pet. 5:7 KJV).

Jesus has changed the lives of millions, myself included. It is interesting that these individuals who call themselves theologians find the truth so disturbing. This reminds us of the conversation between Jesus and Judas regarding the ointment: "Then took Mary a pound of ointment of spikenard, very costly, and anointed the feet of Jesus, and wiped his feet with her hair: and the house was filled with odour of the ointment. Then saith one of his disciples, Judas Iscariot, Simon's *son*, which should betray him. Why was not this ointment sold for three hundred pence, and given to the poor? This he said, not that he cared for the poor; but because he was a thief, and had the bag, and bare what was put therein. Then said Jesus, 'Let her alone: against the day of my burying hath she kept this. For the poor always ye have with you; but me ye have not always' " (John 12:3-8 KJV).

We ask, "Will the liberal theologians ever leave the true Christian alone?" We doubt it! Why? Because, as Jesus forewarned: "Beware of false prophets, which come to you in sheep's clothing, but inwardly they are ravening wolves" (Matt. 7:15 KJV).

It's a terrible shame to put off or reject salvation altogether over an eroneous belief in its conditional nature. That is why this book provides a detailed study of the relevant biblical verses. Feel free to copy portions of this and give it to your friends who have doubts about receiving Jesus into their hearts![12] I remember an orthodox Jewish anti-missionary who sided with liberal "Christians" in an article printed in an anti-missionary article published in the 1980s, when this person began his attack on eternal security, he took New Testament verses out of context to falsely "prove" that a believer could "go to Hell" and "lose" his salvation.

---

[12] We cannot authorize copying of quotes we have obtained permission to use. These quotes are protected by the owners' copyright, and must be written for. However, copying of any of our writings (for the purpose of sharing Jesus—Evangelism) in this 66-page book (as a gift) is permitted and encouraged, with the publisher's address provided. This book is available from the publisher, The Conspiracy, Inc., P.O. Box 12227, Atlanta, Georgia 30355 (1-800-RAM<u>S</u>-HEAD).

The verses he used from the books of Matthew and Hebrews, apply to two different time periods, taken out of context. First, in Matthew, Jesus is explaining to the religious leadership in the presence of his disciples, how utterly impossible it is to work your way to God by the deeds prescribed by the law.

James explains this when he illustrates how difficult the law is to keep: "For whoever keeps the whole law and yet stumbles in one *point*, he has become guilty of all" (James 2:10 NASB). James emphasizes that God looks on the heart, and all men are constantly breaking God's law (Torah) in their hearts. Jesus stressed the importance of this point to explain that only through Himself, the Messiah, could all past, present and future sins be forgiven and paid for (John 14:6; Col. 1:13).

This verse is a testimony to just the opposite of what many liberals claim. These individuals do not even believe the Bible anyway, so why do they present viewpoints in that which they have no belief? The answer is to target and dissuade others to inalienate them from their faith in Jesus. Their false point is that if you believe, you will probably botch it and lose anyway—so why believe in Jesus! They reject the Messiah and they want all others whom they can influence to reject him—misery loves company!

THE VERSE IN HEBREWS ILLUSTRATES A CATCH 22 WHICH UNBELIEVERS DEVISED TO TRAP BELIEVERS

The verse in Hebrews is making references to a practice which emerged in the early Jewish Messianic community. It makes reference to the fact that some believers of that day took up the sacrificial practice again, to escape jailing by Rome. The persecution was brought on by a plan devised by the rabbis and leaders of the Jewish community to punish Messianic Jews. They convinced the Roman authorities that those who believed in the Messiah were enemies[13] of the Roman government. They also suggested how to identify and catch the believers.

These individuals told the Romans that they, as Jews, were obligated to the sacrificial system established within the temple in Jerusalem. They suggested to the Romans that if they would make all Jews buy a certificate of sacrifice purchased for sacrifices offered in the temple, they would be able to identify all who were, under this system, non-Messianic Jews.

The Messianic Jews who realized that Jesus had fulfilled the temple sacrifices ceased to sacrifice and thus were unable to produce this certificate. Hence, when they found a Jew who could not produce the certificate sold by the priest, they caught a Jewish believer in Jesus

---

[13] See Chapter 6 in *The End of History—Messiah Conspiracy Volume I* for documentation on this.

red-handed. Other Jews were promised 10% of all the belongings of Messianic Jews once they denounced them to the Roman authorities.

THE SCARIEST MOST MISUNDERSTOOD VERSE IN THE BIBLE IS SO BECAUSE ITS *ORIGINAL* APPLICATION HAS BEEN LOST FOR 20 CENTURIES

Many Messianic Jews at that time reasoned, "What good am I in jail? I can't spread the word, I can't raise my family and I can't do God's will for my life." So some of them went back under the temple sacrificial system, which Jesus had given his life to fulfill. This clearly was the greatest slap in the face to God since the worshipping of the golden calf in Sinai (Exo. 32:8).

For those who had known better—to go back under the sacrifice of a lamb, which was a prophetic picture of Messiah, once Messiah, himself, had come to pay for sin in full, very nearly[14] was the epitome of blasphemy. This is what the verse means when it says: "...they again crucify to themselves the Son of God, and put Him to open shame" (Heb. 6:6 NASB).

It is not possible for us to do this today[15], since there is no temple left to practice such sacrificial blasphemy against the final work of God through his Messiah (Mark 10:45).[16] We must also remember that the verse does not say "no more salvation," but that forgiveness for the sin doesn't apply when one returns to animal sacrifice in place of the Messiah (Col. 1:14; 2:13).

Jesus having taken **all** your sin out of the way indicates that all those who believe remain forgiven in their past, present and future sins. This is indicated in Ephesians 4:30-32, where it is said that sin grieves the Holy Spirit. A true believer can only grieve the Spirit and bring himself face-to-face with God sooner than God had planned, he cannot send himself to Hell, as some modern day lambasting, Hell-fire and damnation preachers try to tell us.

The scriptures teach us: "If we [believers in Messiah] are faithless, He remains faithful; for He cannot deny Himself" (II Tim. 2:13 NASB; [ ] mine). The ancient Hebrew prophet, Isaiah, wrote seven hundred years before the birth of Jesus: " 'Come now, and let us reason together,' Says the LORD, 'Though your sins are as scarlet, They will be as white as snow; Though they are red like crimson, They will be like wool....' " (Isa. 1:18 NASB).

---

[14]The only worse blasphemy is to reject Jesus by attributing His work to Satan, as some religious leaders did (Matt. 12:22-30). This is the only unforgivable sin, to reject the forgiver, because it negates the very possibility of forgiveness!

[15]In reality, it have not been possible since the temple was destroyed in AD 70. Hebrews was written in AD 68 to the Hebrews (Jews of that day) who were misusing animal sacrifice in a terrible way!

[16]" 'For even the Son of Man did not come to be served, but to serve, and to give His life a ransom for many' " (Mark 10:45 NASB).

THOSE WHO TEACH AGAINST GOD'S TRUTH OF ETERNAL SECURITY, IN THEIR SPIRITUAL INSECURITY, SHOULD BE ASHAMED BECAUSE THEY'VE CAUSED OTHERS TO STUMBLE

So much for those individuals who don't believe, and who, through their own willful insecurity attempt to cause those who believe to stumble and doubt their *eternal salvation*. I believe Jesus spoke of these individuals when he said: "...but whoever causes one of these little ones who believe in Me to stumble, it is better for him that a heavy millstone be hung around his neck, and that he be drowned in the depth of the sea" (Matt. 18:6 NASB).

For those who may have doubts about the biblical truth of eternal security, we recommend you read Dr. Charles Stanley's book, *Eternal Security*,[17] published by Thomas Nelson Publishers. Pastor Stanley is considered by most believers the world over, to have the soundest Bible doctrine one can have! He was twice elected to the presidency of the Southern Baptist Convention and his book is an excellent exposition of the belief that once **saved,** forever saved!!!! And that means always, even to those who mockingly ask us, "Do you believe *Once Saved, Always Saved*?" Yes!

We also suggest you read *The Eternal Safety and Security of all Blood Bought Believers* by Dr. J. M. Carroll[18], and *Eternal Security,* by Arthur W. Pink, published by Baker Book House. Peter Ruckman has authored an excellent book entitled *Eternal Security*[19] Hal Lindsey has a couple of tapes on the question of eternal security, where he proves this issue of biblical doctrine beyond doubt! He has written *Amazing Grace* and *The Guilt Trip*,[20] which also cover this subject. They are available through his tape ministry.[21]

---

[17]In this book, among other issues, Dr. Stanely asks and answers the following three questions: "Think About It: If Christ came to seek and to save that which was lost, and yet we can somehow become unsaved—and therefore undo what Christ came to do—would it not be wise for God to take us on to heaven the moment we are saved in order to insure we make it? Isn't it unnecessarily risky to force us to stay here? .... If our salvation is not secure, how could Jesus say about those to whom He gives eternal life, "and they shall never perish" (John 10:28)? If even one man or woman receives eternal life and then forfeits it through sin or apostasy, will they not perish? And by doing so, do they not make Jesus' words a lie? .... Can joy and insecurity really coexist? How realistic is it to expect us to rejoice over a relationship that is only as secure as our behavior is consistent?" Dr. Charles Stanley, *Eternal Security*, Nashville, TN: Thomas Nelson Inc. © 1990, p. 10, 18, 188.

[18]Available through Bible Baptist Church Publications, Elton Wilson, Pastor, 3102 Prospect Circle, Clarksville, Tennessee 37040

[19]Available through Bible Baptist Bookstore, P.O. Box 7135, Pensacola, Florida 32514.

[20]*The Guilt Trip* is an excerpt of his book *Satan Is Alive And Well On Planet Earth.*

[21]Hal Lindsey Ministries, POB 4000, Palos Verdes, CA, USA 90274. Be sure to ask for the tape "Saved For Eternity".

In an April, 1994, newsletter article, "Once saved, always saved: Is it true?" Hal Lindsey puts it this way: "Salvation is a work of God for man, not a joint work of man and God. Scripture teaches that over and over again. One of the most certain passages on salvation is John 6:37-40. It reads 'All that the Father gives Me will come to Me. And the one who comes to Me, I will never cast out. For I have come down from heaven not to do My own will, but the will of Him who sent Me. And this is the will of Him who sent Me, that of all that He has given Me, I will lose nothing, not even one, but will raise him up on the last day.' So the one who has been given in eternity past by the Father to Christ will come to Him. And the one who comes to Him, He will never cast out. It means once you're in, you will never be cast out."[22]

ETERNAL SECURITY IS THE ULTIMATE REST, PEACE OF MIND AND LICENSE TO SERVE GOD IN BRINGING OUR LOVED ONES INTO HIS FOREVER KINGDOM

A true and honest committed Christian should end each day with a prayer telling the Lord, in so many words, "I know and admit that all I did today was not completely righteous and perfect. I confess[23] those things—even the things I purposely did wrong. I thank You for the blood of Jesus, the Messiah, which covers all those things. And I ask You to fill me anew with Your spirit and to give me the power to follow You even more closely as I continue through life with You. Thank You for Your forgiveness through the redemption Your Messiah purchased for me at Calvary. Amen."

This author could not rest in his Christian life and have any peace of mind until he was convinced of that old "dangerous doctrine", eternal security. It's dangerous all right, but only to Satan. For once someone believes in it, you can't shut him up about Jesus or stop him from giving out the New Testament and biblical literature, and bringing others into God's kingdom!

I want to emphasize here that true believers in Jesus should not view eternal security as a license to sin, but rather as a charter to serve. We find new freedom in being an example to our friends who have not yet accepted eternal life through the Messiah, thus provoking them to jealousy (Rom. 11:11), and thereby bringing them into the eternal kingdom with us, having their best interest at heart!

---

[22]Hal Lindsey, "Hal on the Hot Seat," *Countdown...*, April 1994, used by permission.

[23] I John 1:9 says "If we confess our sins, he is faithful and just to forgive us *our* sins, and to cleanse us from all unrighteousness." "Confess" means simply to agree with God that what you did was not His will. Once you agree the blood of Jesus is reapplied to that particular issue, and you are instantly cleansed and put back into fellowship. Once you confess to the Lord for whatever—your guilt, whether you believe it or not, is dealt with. Jesus took it! Just remind yourself—I am not guilty, Jesus paid—I'm free. Thank you, Lord—and go on! You have no excuse to punish yourself after you say, "I confess."

Thus, we find ourselves sinning less even though we know, technically, if we choose, we can get away with it. That's what I call new life, liberty and freedom. Having the freedom to choose, but in the end choosing for our father, God, and being victorious, because we love him and we know he loves us, even more than our earthly father!

'ÜÏW' PRONOUNCED YESHUA
IS JESUS HEBREW NAME

The **Hebrew code** name, which lights the lamp stand, **is Jesus**. In Hebrew, the shape of the four Hebrew letters spelling Jesus (*Yeshua,* ישׁוע) light God's candelabra, the Jewish menorah![24] This gives us another interesting insight into His true purpose, as found in His vibrant words recorded in the Gospel of John: "I am the **light** of the world; he that followeth me shall not walk in darkness but shall have the light of life" (John 8:12 KJV).

This was foretold seven hundred years before His birth within the Jewish prophetic writings of Isaiah: "And now says the LORD, who formed Me from the womb to be His Servant, To bring Jacob back to Him, in order that Israel might be gathered to Him (For I am honored in the sight of the LORD, And My God is My strength), He says, 'It is too small a thing that You should be My Servant To raise up the tribes of Jacob, and to restore the preserved ones of Israel; I will also make You a **light** of the nations So that My salvation may reach to the end of the earth' (Isaiah 49:5-6 NASB).

---

[24]The menorah, or candlestick, Israel's national symbol, has seven branches (Exodus 25:31). It should not be confused with the *hanukia* menorah, which is used on Hanukkah and has nine branches. Menorah means "lamp" in Hebrew.

"Among the oft-derided Christian literalists, it is said that the Bible is the wholly inspired and inerrant Word of God, and that Holy Spirit guided the mind and hand of its human authors....So-called "higher criticism" and modern linguistic analyses have tended to undercut these claims, critiquing them with what is generally regarded as superior *scientific* method. Few of the methods used, however, meet the rigorous criteria of hard science and mathematical statistics. In 1988 an obscure paper was published—in a prominent, rigorous, indeed premier, scientific journal—with results that may demolish the claims of the "higher" critics...The paper... entitled "Equidistant Letter Sequences in the Book of Genesis"...was published in the eminent *Journal of the Royal Statistical Society*....mathematical statisticians, discovered words encoded into the Hebrew text that could not have been accidental—nor placed there by human hand...the authors...found that some pairs of words were predictive—that is, they could not have been known to the supposedly human authors of the Hebrew text because they occurred long after the Bible was composed....This in effect is what the researchers have found embedded in the Hebrew text of the Torah—a whole series of meaningful word-pairs in close proximity, something that they demonstrate cannot have happened by chance. These words they found in close proximity are not simply the words of the text (as would be the case in the analogy above of an unknown potential language). They were rather words composed of letters selected at various equal skip distances, for example, every second or third or fourth letter. It was as though "behind" the surface meaning of the Hebrew there was a second, hidden level of embedded meaning....such word-pairs still occurred much too frequently to be accounted for by chance. And other combinations also appear so often that it begins to look not so much like a random happening, but like something carefully embedded in the text. For example, the researchers also found the pair Zedekiah (a sixth century B.C.E. kind of Judah), and Matanya, Zedekiah's original name (see 2 Kings 24:17); and the pair Hanukkah (the Jewish festival that commemorates the re-dedication of the Temple after it was recaptured from the Assyrians in the second century B.C.E.) and Hasmoneans (the family name of the leaders of the Jewish forces that managed to wrest the Temple from the Assyrian monarch Antiochus IV Epiphanes). Note that these names and events found encoded in the text of the Torah involved people who lived, and events that occurred, long after the Torah was composed, whether by a divine or human hand....The published results show that this finding was significant at a level of 1.8×10^{17}, that is, the odds of its occurring merely by chance are less than 1 in 50 quadrillion. (A quadrillion is one with 15 zeros after it.) A finding in most scientific journals is considered significant at chance levels of anything less than 1 in 20. The capacity to embed so many, meaningfully related, randomly selected word-pairs in a body of text with a coherent surface meaning is stupendously beyond the intellectual capacity of any human being or group of people, however brilliant, and equally beyond the capacity of any conceivable computing device....the phenomenon....could...[not] be found in other texts, sacred or otherwise. One of the reviewers had them try the same test on Tolstoy's *War and Peace*; so the researchers chose a section of the Hebrew translation that was the same length as Genesis, but the phenomenon did not appear in *War and Peace*."[1]

Jeffrey B. Satinover, 1995

APPENDIX 1
HEBREW BIBLE
CODES AUTHENTICATE
THE SCRIPTURE AS GOD'S WORD!

We realize that many who may read this book validating the truth of eternal security, who may not believe the Bible is God's word, may

---

[1]Jeffrey B. Satinover, "Divine Authorship? Computer Reveals Startling Word Patterns", *Bible Review*, © Oct. 1995, pp. 28-31, 44, used by permission. [ ] mine.

comment, "Well, this is all fine and dandy, but how do I know there is a God and I need to be saved by Him through His Messiah, Jesus?" (The following four framed page displays are inserted to validate the statement "Rabbis of ancient times ... rightly interpreted this prophecy [Isaiah 52-3] to refer to the Messiah ..." on page 20⇨)

ORIGINAL HEBREW TEXT WRITTEN 712 BC

הִנֵּה יַשְׂכִּיל עַבְדִּי יָרוּם וְנִשָּׂא וְגָבַהּ מְאֹד:

ישעיה נב:יג

OLD TESTAMENT SCRIPTURE TRANSLATION

"Behold, My servant will prosper, He will be high and lifted up, and greatly exalted."   **Isaiah 52:13 NASB**

ANCIENT RABBINICAL COMMENTARY

"Behold, my servant, the Messiah, shall prosper; he shall be exalted, etc. 'Behold, my servant shall deal prudently.' This is the King Messiah. 'He shall be exalted and extolled, and be very high.' He shall be exalted more than Abraham; for of Him it is written, 'I have exalted my hand to the Lord' (Gen. XIV.22). He shall be extolled more than Moses....(Num. XI.12)."[2]

Targum

NEW TESTAMENT RECORDED 90 AD

"...as Moses lifted up the serpent in the wilderness, even so must the Son of Man be lifted up; that whoever believes may in Him have eternal life....'When you lift up the Son of Man, then you will know that I am *He*, and I do nothing on My own initiative, but I speak these things as the Father taught Me.' "

John 3:14-15; 8:28 NASB

MODERN RABBINIC COMMENT/REFUTATION

"...the Christians assert, that the prophecy of Isaiah constitutes a prediction of Jesus, the Nazarene, concerning whom Isaiah has said, 'He shall be exalted and extolled, and be very high,' because to him alone it is asserted these words can be attributed....The word יַשְׂכִּיל 'he shall prosper,' is found again in the 1st Samuel xviii. 14, 'And David *was prosperous* in all ways.' 'My servant shall prosper,' relates to that period when Israel shall leave the countries of its captivity, and be elevated to the highest degree of happiness."

Faith Strengthened, by Isaac Troki, pp. 108-118; 1850

AUTHOR'S COMMENT—EVANGELICAL CHRISTIAN POSITION

Isaac Troki's refutation of the Messianic interpretation and application of Isaiah 52:13 clearly flies in the face of the ancient rabbinical understanding. As you see, the Jewish Targum of many centuries past definitely explains this biblical passage to be about the Messiah. On the other hand, our Christian polemic friend would have us believe that it is about Israel's happiness. That's a new one on us. When Mr. Troki said, "The Christians assert," he was apparently ignorant of the fact that the Targum also "asserted"—Messiah! Right? Yes!

Philip Moore

---

[2]Rev. B. Pick, Ph.D., *Old Testament Passages Messianically Applied by the Ancient Synagogue*, published in the compilation *Hebraica, A Quarterly Journal in the Interests of Semitic Study*, Vol. I, New York: Charles Scribner's Sons, 1886-88, p. 268.

ORIGINAL HEBREW TEXT WRITTEN 712 B.C.

לָכֵן אֲחַלֶּק־לֹו בָרַבִּים וְאֶת־עֲצוּמִים יְחַלֵּק שָׁלָל תַּחַת אֲשֶׁר הֶעֱרָה לַמָּוֶת נַפְשֹׁו
וְאֶת־פֹּשְׁעִים נִמְנָה וְהוּא חֵטְא־רַבִּים נָשָׂא וְלַפֹּשְׁעִים יַפְגִּיעַ:
ישעיה נג:יב

OLD TESTAMENT SCRIPTURE TRANSLATION

"Therefore, I will allot Him a portion with the great, And He will divide the booty with the strong; Because He poured out Himself to death, And was numbered with the transgressors; Yet He Himself bore the sin of many, And interceded for the transgressors." **Isaiah 53:12 NASB**

ANCIENT RABBINICAL COMMENTARY

"And when Israel is sinful, the MESSIAH seeks for mercy upon them, as it is written, 'By His Stripes we were healed, and HE carried the sins of many; and MADE INTERCESSION FOR THE TRANSGRESSORS.' "[3]
B'reshith Rabban, pp. 430, 671

NEW TESTAMENT RECORDED 57 AND 63 AD

"For even the Son of Man did not come to be served, but to serve, and to give His life a ransom for many....For I tell you, that this which is written must be fulfilled in Me, 'AND HE WAS NUMBERED WITH TRANSGRESSORS'; for that which refers to Me has *its* fulfillment." **Mark 10:45; Luke 22:37 NASB**

MODERN RABBINIC COMMENT/REFUTATION

"Isaiah 53:1-8 finds the prophet quoting the astonished exclamations of the Gentile spokesmen....In the latter part of verse 10 through verse 12, the prophet records the blessings with which God will reward His faithful servant for all the abuse and injury he endured for the sanctification of the Name of God....the servant, Israel, formerly despised by the nations, will now attain a place of honor and recognition among 'the great,' the sovereign nations of the world...."
The Jew and the Christian Missionary, by Gerald Sigal, pp. 37, 64; 1981

AUTHOR'S COMMENT—EVANGELICAL CHRISTIAN POSITION

Where Gerald Sigal, under the direction of Rabbi Bronznick, gets the idea that Isaiah 53 concerns a "Gentile spokesman," eludes us. It would also have eluded the most brilliant ancient Jewish rabbinical commentators. This Messianic passage in Isaiah begins with: "Who hath believed **our** [Hebrew prophetic Jewish] report? and to **whom** is the arm of the LORD revealed?" (Isa. 53:1 KJV; [ ] mine). We all, even most rabbis and nominal "Christians," agree that it was the Jews who wrote the Old Testament in the midst of a pagan world as God's revelation to man. Further, Isaiah, who said *He bore our sorrows*, is Jewish! We believe Gerald Sigal and Rabbi Bronznick should read the ancient Jewish commentaries we have quoted, in their original Hebrew, if they know enough Hebrew. This passage cannot refer to Israel as implied by our friendly Jewish *Christian polemicist*. Though Israel will be sovereign when Jesus returns and establishes the millennium, this passage, as indicated by the ancient rabbinical commentary, refers to the Messiah, one who would be punished and beaten while praying for His enemies. This was never true of Israel but was true of Jesus! Furthermore, the Jewish Targum Jonathan to Isaiah 43:10-12, emphatically states that this servant is the *Messiah*. It says: " 'You are witnesses before Me,' says the Lord, 'and My servant is the Messiah, whom I have chosen; that you may know and believe Me, and that you may understand that I am He who was from the beginning, and also that all eternities belong to Me, and besides Me there is no God.' "[4]   **Philip Moore**

---

[3]F. Kenton Beshore, D.D., LL.D., Ph.D., *"The Messiah" of the Targums, Talmuds and Rabbinical Writers*, Los Angeles, CA: World Bible Society, 1971, pp. chart 26.
[4]Samson H. Levey, *The Messiah: An Aramaic Interpretation, The Messianic Exegesis of the Targum*, Jerusalem: Hebrew Union College/Jewish Institute of Religion, 1974, p. 62.

ORIGINAL HEBREW TEXT WRITTEN 712 BC

אָכֵן חֳלָיֵנוּ הוּא נָשָׂא וּמַכְאֹבֵינוּ סְבָלָם וַאֲנַחְנוּ חֲשַׁבְנֻהוּ נָגוּעַ מֻכֵּה אֱלֹהִים וּמְעֻנֶּה:

ישעיה נג:ד

OLD TESTAMENT SCRIPTURE TRANSLATION

"Surely our griefs He Himself bore, And our sorrows He carried; Yet we ourselves esteemed Him stricken, Smitten of God, and afflicted."

Isaiah 53:4 NASB

ANCIENT RABBINICAL COMMENTARY

"The rabbis say, His name is the leper of the house of Rabbi, as it is said, 'Surely he hath borne our sickness, and endured the burden of our pains, yet we did esteem him stricken, smitten of God, and afflicted' (Isa. LIII., 4)."[5]

Sanhedrin, fol. 98, col 2

NEW TESTAMENT RECORDED 60 AD

"...He Himself [Jesus] bore our sins in His body on the cross...for by His wounds you were healed. For you were continually straying like sheep, but now you have returned to the Shepherd and Guardian of your souls."

I Peter 2:24 NASB. [ ] mine

MODERN RABBINIC COMMENT/REFUTATION

"In verse 4 [of Isa. 53], the Gentile spokesmen depict the servant as bearing the 'diseases' and carrying the 'pains' which they themselves should have suffered. At the time of the servant's suffering, the Gentiles believed that the servant was undergoing divine retribution for *his* sins....we must conclude that this statement, made by the enemies of the suffering servant of the Lord, does not refer to Jesus, who, it is alleged, suffered as an atonement for mankind's sins. There is no indication in this verse that the servant of God suffered to atone for the sins of others....This is the confession of the Gentile spokesmen, who now realize that it was they and their people who deserved to suffer the humiliations inflicted on the servant of the Lord, as they stated in verses 4-6."

The Jew and the Christian Missionary,
by Gerald Sigal, pp. 42-43, 52; © 1981. [ ] mine

AUTHOR'S COMMENT—EVANGELICAL CHRISTIAN POSITION

See our comments on previous Isaiah 53 comparison on page 17.

Philip Moore

---

[5]Rev. B. Pick, Ph.D., *Old Testament Passages Messianically Applied by the Ancient Synagogue*, published in the compilation *Hebraica, A Quarterly Journal in the Interests of Semitic Study*, Vol. II, p. 27.

The three previous comparison page illustrations demonstrate that the Rabbis reinterpreted the Messiah, and those biblical passages which Judaism had always said were predictive of his then future suffering. For twenty-five hundred years, the Jews have recited the above eighteen benediction amidah blessings on the Sabbath in their synagogues. Mysteriously, after AD 80, the twelfth blessing of these eighteen was altered! A curse against Jewish believers in Jesus was added to oust the Messianic Jews from the synagogue to keep them from telling other Jews about the Jewish prophecies of Jesus. The twelfth prayer was altered to read, in part, "may the *nôzrîm* [Jewish Christians, i.e., Messianic Jews] and *mînîm* be destroyed in a moment."[6] In Hebrew, "והנוצרים והמינים יכלו כרגע"[7] The Schechter fragment above, with the word nozrim circled by this author, was only discovered in 1925 and reveals the Jewish Christians were numerous and considered a threat! When the twelfth of these eighteen prayers were recited by the congregation in the synagogue, the Messianic believers would be silent, not willing to curse themselves. Thus they were then detected, and later asked to leave by the leadership. Centuries later, there was no trace of this prayer and some Jewish scholars vainly deny it was used for this purpose. Very few laymen know it ever existed! In todays Jewish prayer books, the word *nôzrîm,* i.e., Nazarenes, is replaced with the word "slanderers". No hint of an anti-Jewish Christian conspiracy is thus revealed. It has been kept under wraps for centuries. See our *The End of History—Messiah Conspiracy,* Vol. I, chapters 7-9 for over 100 pages of documentation on this subject. Photo of fragment T-S.8.H.24[5] courtesy of Syndics of Cambridge University Library.

---

[6] Ray A. Pritz, *Nazarene Jewish Christianity,* Jerusalem: The Magness Press, Hebrew University, 1988, p. 104, [ ] mine, used by permission.
[7] Ibid.

⊳ We are glad you asked, "Why, God? Why, Messiah?" In recent years, critical Hebrew Bible codes have been and are being discovered within biblical text.

To illustrate that every letter of the Scripture in its original language, is inspired by God Himself. We present the following codes, of which it is obvious no man could have penned outside of divine inspiration!

THE NAME OF JESUS IS MYSTERIOUSLY ENCODED
IN ISAIAH'S PROPHECY ABOUT THE MESSIAH

In the latter portions of Isaiah 52 and all of chapter 53, we are introduced to the suffering servant of the Lord. Many **rabbis of ancient times**, along with the New Testament, rightly **interpreted this prophecy to refer to the Messiah**, as you previously read.

When we take the fascinating phenomenon of the original Hebrew and count out every eighth word starting at the first *ude* in verse 13 of Isaiah 52, we discover that the Hebrew letters spell Jesus' name! In the Bible, the number eight symbolizes new beginnings. Jesus brought us the New Covenant/New Testament (new beginnings) predicted by Jeremiah. Interesting, wouldn't you say? Below, we enlarge the letters which spell the name of Jesus (Hebrew is read from right to left).

כִּי לֹא בְחִפָּזוֹן תֵּצֵאוּ וּבִמְנוּסָה לֹא תֵלֵכוּן כִּי־הֹלֵךְ לִפְנֵיכֶם יְהוָה וּמְאַסִפְכֶם אֱלֹהֵי יִשְׂרָאֵל:
הִנֵּה יַשְׂכִּיל עַבְדֵּי יָרוּם וְנִשָּׂא וְגָבַה מְאֹד: כַּאֲשֶׁר שָׁמְמוּ עָלֶיךָ רַבִּים כֵּן־מִשְׁחַת
מֵאִישׁ מַרְאֵהוּ וְתֹאֲרוֹ מִבְּנֵי אָדָם: כֵּן יַזֶּה גּוֹיִם רַבִּים עָלָיו יִקְפְּצוּ מְלָכִים פִּיהֶם
כִּי אֲשֶׁר לֹא־סֻפַּר לָהֶם רָאוּ וַאֲשֶׁר לֹא־שָׁמְעוּ הִתְבּוֹנָנוּ:

Isaiah 52: 12-15
יֵשׁוּעַ = Jesus

The above words with their first letter in bold type are translated as: יַשְׂכִּיל "he will deal wisely"; שָׁמְמוּ "they shall be astonished"; וְתֹאֲרוֹ "and his appearance"; עָלָיו "concerning him." Here you have the key meaning of salvation, and the Jews' response to Jesus' wisdom in giving Himself for their atonement, astonishment. Today, as we tell Jews about Jesus and show them these prophecies, they are indeed astonished.

THE NAME OF GOD IS ENCODED
IN HIS ACCOUNT OF CREATION IN GENESIS

Likewise, *Yahweh* (Yehovah) is spelled out in Hebrew at twenty-two letter intervals[8] (there are twenty-two letters in the Hebrew

---

[8]There are exactly twenty-two letters between the letters in bold type.

alphabet). This is the ancient and most holy name of God, encoded in
the beginning verses of His account of creation.

בְּרֵאשִׁית בָּרָא אֱלֹהִים אֵת הַשָּׁמַיִם וְאֵת הָאָרֶץ: וְהָאָרֶץ הָיְתָה תֹהוּ וָבֹהוּ וְחֹשֶׁךְ עַל־פְּנֵי
תְהוֹם וְרוּחַ אֱלֹהִים מְרַחֶפֶת עַל־פְּנֵי הַמָּיִם: וַיֹּאמֶר אֱלֹהִים יְהִי אוֹר וַיְהִי־אוֹר: וַיַּרְא
אֱלֹהִים אֶת־ הָאוֹר כִּי־טוֹב וַיַּבְדֵּל אֱלֹהִים בֵּין הָאוֹר וּבֵין הַחֹשֶׁךְ: וַיִּקְרָא אֱלֹהִים ׀
לָאוֹר יוֹם וְלַחֹשֶׁךְ קָרָא לָיְלָה וַיְהִי־עֶרֶב וַיְהִי־בֹקֶר יוֹם אֶחָד:

Genesis 1:1-5

יהוה = Yahweh/God

DECODING THE MESSIANIC MYSTERY OF
THE FIRST TEN NAMES IN HEBREW HISTORY

We would like to point out that the very meanings of the Jewish
names of our original ancestors reveal God's plan to send His suffering
Messiah, as a mortal, who would die for us.

Missler points out that: "In Hebrew: *Adam* (אָדָם) means 'man';
Seth (שֵׁת) means 'appointed'; *Enosh* (אֱנוֹשׁ) means 'mortal'; *Kenan* (קֵינָן)
means 'sorrow'; *Mahalalel* (מַהֲלַלְאֵל) means 'the blessed God'; *Jared*
(יֶרֶד) means 'shall come down'; *Enoch* (חֲנוֹךְ) means 'teaching';
Methuselah (מְתוּשֶׁלַח) means 'his death shall bring'; *Lamech* (לֶמֶךְ)
means 'the despairing'; and *Noah* (נֹחַ) means 'rest' or 'comfort.' "[9]

Reading this genealogy of names as a sentence, translating them
from Hebrew to English, we get: "Man is appointed mortal sorrow.
The blessed God shall come down, teaching that his death shall bring
the despairing comfort." This, indirectly but clearly, shows that the
God Incarnate Messiah would give His life for us, as Jesus did.

PRIME MINISTER RABIN'S ASSASSINATION—
ENCODED IN THE VERY PROMISE HE VIOLATED?

Some Jews feel that key Scriptures indicate Rabin's assassination
was foreseen in the Bible. In Genesis 15:17-18 we find God's
covenant of the land of Israel to Abraham; it reads: "And it came
about when the sun had set, that it was very dark, and behold, *there
appeared* a smoking oven and a flaming torch which passed between
these pieces. On that day the LORD made a covenant with Abram,
saying, 'To your descendants I have given this land, From the river of
Egypt as far as the great river, the river Euphrates....' " (NASB).

---

[9]Chuck Missler, "Mystery of the Messiah." Coeur d'Alene, ID: Koinonia House, ©
1994, used by permission. ( ) mine. Audio tape available through Koinonia House, POB
D, Coeur d'Alene, ID, USA 83816-0347. The following translation, ibid.

The word "fire" in Hebrew is *esh* (אֵשׁ). *Lapide* means "fire
torch" (לַפִּיד). *Avar* (עָבַר) means "passed," and *bean* (בֵּין) means
"between." If you take the last letter of *avar* (ר), which is "r," and
combine it with the word *bean*, you have the name Rabin (רבִּין), who
was, in fact, killed by gun*fire* passing between his body, for attempting
to give away large amounts of land God gave to Abraham and his
people (עָבַר בֵּין).

Once we combine the last letter "r" of עָבַר to spell Rabin with the
next word, the remaining two words at the beginning of the sentence
once the r of Ashar is also moved forward onto the (ע) ine of avar spell
"fire" (*esh*), Fire fire ra רַע (bad) so in two words where the last letter of
one is joined to the first of the next word, you form three new words,
which read, literally, "fire bad rabin." Genesis 15:9-10 mentioned
animals that were sacrificed and set apart, then the fire passed between
the pieces, sealing the covenant between God and Abraham, the father
of the Jewish people. Some Orthodox Jews feel Rabin was sacrificed
so that the covenant between the land and the people God made would
not be broken.

On a closer examination of this verse, we observed additional
similarities. The Bible mentions that the fire passed between the
sacrifices after the sun went down. It was also after the sun went down
that Rabin was fired upon. What is even more interesting is that if you
read this line of Genesis 15:17, אֵשׁ אֲשֶׁר עָבַר בֵּין, (esh ashar avar bean)
with the first "b" (בֵּ) removed as אֵשׁ אֵשׁ רַע רַבֵּין, it translates *esh esh ra
rabin*, which means "fire, fire, bad rabin." The numerical equivalent of
"b" in Hebrew is two; this was Rabin's second time in office.

Reading left to right, as we do in Hebrew, the passage breaks
down literally:

Rabin בֵּין ר two בֵּ bad עָ ר fire אֲשֶׁר fire אֵשׁ,

Prime Minister Rabin was hit with gun*fire twice* when he was
assassinated, and was considered to be *bad* by his assassin and many
religious Jews, who felt he was violating the biblical Scriptures by
giving away important areas of the land of Israel in the name of peace.
When Isaac Rabin's initials (Ude-e or i and Resh-r), the first and last
letters are removed from the assassin's name, Egal Amir, reads Gal
Ami, "Redeemer of My People," i.e., National Hero in Hebrew.

The Jews have a different weekly portion of the law of Moses
they read every week, year in and year out, the world over in their
synagogues. Believe it or not, the portion which was read in the
synagogue services the week Rabin was shot included this line in
Genesis 15!

In the Bible, forty represents judgment. The Israelites were forty years in the desert. For example, Noah was in the ark for forty days and forty nights while the world was underwater. Likewise, Rabin was buried on the fortieth day after he signed the Oslo Agreement in Washington DC, which handed key Israeli cities in the West Bank over to the Arabs, which violates God's covenant with Abraham. God's[10] consequences???

GAON AND JESUS ON THE DIVINE INSPIRATION
OF THE BIBLE'S HEBREW TEXT

Recently, in the October 1995 *Bible Review* article entitled, "Divine Authorship? Computer reveals startling word patterns" (concerning inspired mathematical Bible codes, we quoted on page 15), it was noted that: "....The paper, by Doron Witzturn, Eliyahu Rips and Yoav Rosenberg of the Jerusalem College of Technology and the Hebrew University, is innocuously entitled 'Equidistant Letter Sequences in the Book of Genesis'...Following publication of this paper, a public statement was issued, signed by five mathematical scholars—two from Harvard, two from Hebrew University and one from Yale. 'The present work,' they said, 'represents serious research carried out by serious investigators....results obtained are sufficiently striking to deserve a wider audience and to encourage further study.' The work was also critiqued and endorsed by Dr. Andrew Goldfinger, a senior research physicist at Johns Hopkins University in Baltimore, and by Harold Gans, an analyst with the U.S. Department of Defense.

According to Jewish tradition, the Torah contains all knowledge; therefore the codes embedded in the Torah also encompass information that transcends the limitation of time. The Vilna Gaon, the great 18th century Rabbi of Vilna, Lithuania, a child prodigy and one of the most brilliant men in Jewish history, wrote that 'all that was, is, and will be unto the end of time is included in the Torah...and not merely in a general sense, but including the details of every species and of each person individually, and the most minute details of everything that happened to him from the day of his birth until his death.'

Some may be reminded of the words of the Rabbi from Nazareth [Jesus], seen in a different light: 'I tell you the truth, until heaven and earth disappear, not the smallest letter [literally *iota*, equivalent to the Hebrew *yod*, the smallest letter in the Hebrew alphabet], not the least stroke of a pen [literally *tittle*, a reference to the small decoration or 'crown' on some Hebrew letters in handwritten scrolls of the Torah],

---

[10] While we condemn the act of murder and the tragedy brought to Rabin's family, we dare not stand in judgement of God. If Rabin was acting contrary to the will of God, and knew he was doing so, the author of life, who gave life, reserves the right to take it. In Psalm 68:20 it is written "...unto God the Lord belongs the issues from death." Perhaps God removed his protective hand from Rabin when he refused to heed His biblical injunction He gave to Abraham in Genesis 15.

will by any means disappear from the Torah [Law] until everything is accomplished' (Matthew 5:18)....The phenomenon [the Hebrew equidistant letter sequences spelling encoded and relevant words applicable to the surface text of the Bible] cannot be attributed to anything within the known physical universe, human beings included. Moreover, rigorous proof of the existence and validity of the phenomenon requires both high-speed computation and only recently developed techniques of statistical analysis....What then was the purpose of encoding this information into the text? Some would say it is the Author's signature. Is it His way of assuring us that at this particular, late moment—when our scientific, materialistic doubt has reached its apotheosis, when we have been driven to the brink of radical skepticism—that He is *precisely* who He had said He is in that astonishing, radical core document of the Judeo-Christian tradition?"[11]

נִשְׁבַּע יְהוָה וְלֹא יִנָּחֵם אֲדֹנָי אַתָּה־כֹהֵן

לְעוֹלָם, עַל־דִּבְרָתִי מַלְכִּי־צֶדֶק :

Circled are a *ude* and *tittle* in Hebrew text, to which Jesus referred.

Codes on pages 20-22 and illustrations in this appendix were not included in the article in *Bible Review* or the paper mentioned therein.

Publications, such as the *Los Angeles Times, Atlanta Journal and Constitution* and *Time,* featured headlines regarding newly discovered, yet repressed, Dead Sea Scroll evidence. This evidence supports the suffering role of the Messiah, and hints at the fact that these very same things happened to Jesus during this time period (see our Volume I, Chapter 24 for details on the Dead Sea Scrolls and Jesus).

---

[11]Jeffrey B. Satinover, "Divine Authorship? Computer reveals startling word patterns", *Bible Review*, © Oct. 1995, pp. 28, 44-45, used by permission. First [ ] mine. Second and third [ ] are my insertion of the article's footnotes to Jesus' words, *letter*, and *pen*. Fifth [ ] mine. In *Nightmare of the Apocalypse*, I present additional Hebrew Bible codes.

"R. Shim'on said to them: 'It is not the will of the Holy O`ne, blessed be He, that too much be revealed to the world. But when the days of the Messiah approach, even the children of the world will be able to discover secrets of wisdom, and to know through them the Ends and the Calculations...."[1]   Zohar 1:117b-118a

"For thus saith the LORD of hosts; Yet once, it *is* a little while, and I will shake the heavens, and the earth, and the sea, and the dry *land*; And I will shake all nations, and the **desire**[2] of all nations shall come...."   Haggai 2:6-7 KJV

"And there shall be signs in the sun, and in the moon, and in the stars; and upon the earth distress of nations, with perplexity; the sea and the waves roaring; Men's hearts failing them for fear, and for looking after those things which are coming on the earth: for the powers of heaven shall be shaken....And when these things begin to come to pass, then look up, and lift up your heads; for your redemption draweth nigh."   Jesus—Luke 21:25-26, 28 KJV

"...our Forefathers wrongfully put [him] [Jesus] to death and that Sin lies upon us unto this day."[3]   Rabbi Nathan Shapira of Jerusalem, 1657

"...radioactive poisoning of the atmosphere, and hence, annihilation of any life on earth, has been brought within the range of technical possibility."[4]   Albert Einstein, warning of the results of the imminent development of the hydrogen bomb

"In my opinion....We must aim at a stable state society and the destruction of nuclear stockpiles. Otherwise, I don't see how we can survive much later than 2050."[5]   Dr. Jacques Monod, French molecular biologist

APPENDIX 2
A REVIEW OF MESSIAH'S SECOND COMING IN LIGHT OF TODAY'S RABBINICAL OPPOSITION

In this section, we will paraphrase and excerpt some material from *Volume I*, regarding the Messiah's Second Coming, to illustrate our firm conviction that the rabbis are in error in their claim that Jesus is *not the Messiah*, as was presented earlier on pages 16-18.

In the following pages, we document that they have been mistaken every time during the past two millennial aeons, in relation to their speculation of the Messiah's arrival. Thus, since they are not infallible, perhaps they are also wrong in their "case-closed" position, with regard to considering Jesus' eligibility as the Messiah.

---

[1]Raphael Patai, *The Messiah Texts*, Detroit: Wayne State University Press, © 1979, p. 63.
[2]Desire, in this passage, refers to the Messiah, Jesus Christ.
[3]Richard Popkin/Gordon Weiner, eds., *Jewish Christians and Christian Jews*, Boston: Kluwer Academic Publishers, © 1994, p. 65. Second [ ] mine.
[4]"Einstein," *Nova*, 1976. The hydrogen bomb was developed shortly after Einstein made this comment, though as of this date, it has never been used in warfare.
[5]Josh McDowell, *Prophecy, Fact or Fiction*, San Bernardino, Here's Life Pub., 1981, p. 3.

A WORLD OF MESSIANIC MISTAKES AND ERRORS

There are many examples which illustrate just how often Jewish leaders and rabbis have been mistaken in dating the Coming of the Messiah! Nearly 2000 years ago, Rabbi Yohanan Ben Zakkai felt the Messiah would be coming in his time.[6] Rabbi Jose, the Galilean, said the Messiah would come in 130 AD. Rabbi Eleazar ben Azariah predicted He would come in 140 AD. Rabbi Judah ha-Nasi (c. 135-220), redactor of the Mishnah, said 435 AD would be the date of His Coming. Rabbi Hanina of the third century said He would be here by 470 AD. Rabbi Elazar ben Arak maintained Messiah would come in 620 AD. Salmon ben Yeroham (a Karaite) thought He would be here in 968 AD. Judah Halevi, poet and author of *Kuzari* (1080-1141), said 1130 AD would be the date for the Messiah.[7] Rabbi Moshe ben Maimon (the great Rambam; 1135-1204) set the date for the Coming of the Messiah at 1210 AD.[8] Rabbi Abraham bar Hiyya, who died in 1136, said 1230 AD.[9] Abraham ben Alexander of Cologne, author of *Keter Shem Tov*, and the mid-thirteenth century student of Eliazar of Worms "gives the year 1329 as the Messianic year."[10]

The French Rabbi Levi ben Abraham (c. 1240-1315) gave 1345 AD as the Messianic year in his manuscript, *Liwyat Hen*. Levi ben Gershon (1288-1344), known to us as Gersonides, maintained 1358 AD was the date. Benjamin Ben Moses Nahawendi (the great Karaite of the eighth and ninth centuries) insisted 1358 AD would be the time.[11] Rabbi Sh'lomo ben Yitzhay (the great and famed Rashi; 1040-1105) set the Messiah's date of arrival at 1352 AD.[12] Rabbi Moshe ben Nahman (the well-known Nahmanides; 1194-1268) predicted a date of 1403 AD.[13]   Joseph ben Isaac Bekor Shor (French Tosafist/exegete) and Bahya ben Asher of Saragossa, both said 1403.[14]

Abraham Halevi, a Cabbalist who was exiled from Spain in the sixteenth century, wrote in his 1508 commentary on Daniel, *Mashre Kitrin* (The Loosener of Knots), that the Messiah would come in 1530. Italian Rabbi Mordecai ben Judah Dato (1527-1585), who wrote

[6]Raphael Patai, *The Messiah Texts*, p. 54.
[7]Abba Hillel Silver, D.D., *A History of Messianic Speculation in Israel, from the First through the Seventeenth Centuries*. New York: The MacMillan Company, 1927, pp. 20, 25-26, 40, 52, 68.
[8]Raphael Patai, *The Messiah Texts*, p. 55. There are many who deny that Rambam set a date. You are free to consider Patai's evidence and decide for yourself.
[9]Abba Hillel Silver, D.D., *A History of Messianic Speculation in Israel*, pp. 69-71.
[10]Ibid, p. 99.
[11]Ibid, pp. 99-100, 94, 55.
[12]Raphael Patai, *The Messiah Texts*, p. 55.
[13]Abba Hillel Silver, D.D., *A History of Messianic Speculation in Israel*, pp. 83-84.
[14]Ibid, pp. 66, 94, 96-97.

Migdal David, was of the conviction that the Messiah would come in 1575. Eliezer Ashkenazi ben Eli Rofe (d. 1586), who wrote *Ma'ase Adonai,* a commentary on the Pentateuch, offered 1594 as "the Messianic year." Gedalia ibn Yahya, in his book *Sefer Shalshelet ha-Kabbala,* suggested 1598. Even one hundred and ten-year-old David ben Solomon ibn Abi Zimra (1479-1589), who wrote *Magen David,* a mystical interpretation of the Hebrew alphabet, said He would come in 1640.[15] Rabbi Moses de Leon (1240-1305), Isaiah Horowitz (1555-1630), and Yom-Tov Lippmann Heller, all three, said 1648 was the date.[16]

Isaac Cohen, who published *Pa'aneah Raza* in 1607, said 1713-14 was pristine, the perfect date. Rabbi Nathan Nata Spira (c. 1584-1633) of Cracow said 1725. Rabbi Simeon ben Zemah Duran (1361-1444), who wrote *Oheb Mishpat,* a commentary on Job, gave the year of 1850.

Rabbi Samuel ben Judah Velerio, physician and biblical commentator, who died in the second half of the sixteenth century after writing *Hazon la-Mo'ed,* said 1868 was the Messiah's date.[17] Rabbi Meir Loeb ben Y'hiel Mikhael Malbim (1809-1879), who was the chief rabbi of Rumania, said 1913.[18] Joseph ben David ibn Yahya (the fourth; 1494-1539) said the Messiah would come in the year 1931.[19]

In the early 1980's we spoke to more than one rabbi in Israel who felt that because the Hebrew spelling of the Jewish year, which would occur in 1984, was *Tishmad,* meaning "destruction," that would be the year. Needless to say, we were unable to convince them until 1985, that this date, too, was in error.

Rabbi Schneerson, leader of the Jewish Lubovitcher movement and thought to be the Messiah by some, predicted that the Messiah would come by September 9, 1991.[20] He did not, and the rabbi died in June 1994, which dashed the hopes of many! The truth of the matter is that Jesus is the Messiah who will come **again**! Many in Judaism deny that there is a **Jewish teaching** that the Messiah will come **twice**—they are wrong. We expose this error with the following quotes and comparisons.

---

[15]Abba Hillel Silver, D.D., *A History of Messianic Speculation in Israel,* pp. 130, 135, 139-142.

[16]Raphael Patai, *The Messiah Texts,* pp. 55-56.

[17]Abba Hillel Silver, D.D., *A History of Messianic Speculation in Israel,* pp. 186-187, 107, 143.

[18]Raphael Patai, *The Messiah Texts,* p. 56.

[19]Abba Hillel Silver, D.D., *A History of Messianic Speculation in Israel,* p. 142.

[20]Don Lattin, "Jewish Sect is Expecting Its Messiah by Sept. 9." *San Francisco Chronicle,* Apr. 15, 1991, p. 5.

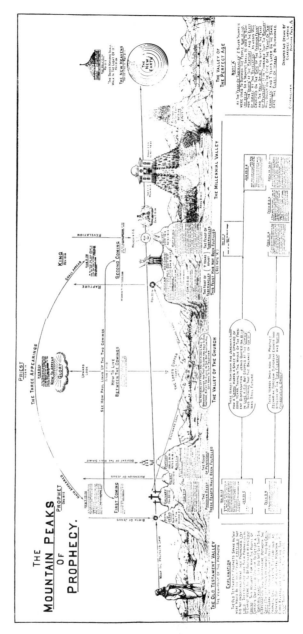

A chart by Rev. Clarence Larkin illustrating the mountain peaks
of prophecy regarding the Messiah's two Comings.[21]

[21] Chart courtesy of Rev. Clarence Larkin Estate, from the book *Dispensational Truth*.
Available through Rev. Clarence Larkin, Est., POB 334 Glenside, PA, USA 19038.

ORIGINAL HEBREW TEXT WRITTEN 780 BC

אֵלֵךְ אָשׁוּבָה אֶל־מְקוֹמִי עַד אֲשֶׁר־יֶאְשְׁמוּ וּבִקְשׁוּ פָנַי בַּצַּר לָהֶם יְשַׁחֲרֻנְנִי׃ לְכוּ וְנָשׁוּבָה
אֶל־יְהוָה כִּי הוּא טָרָף וְיִרְפָּאֵנוּ יָךְ וְיַחְבְּשֵׁנוּ׃ יְחַיֵּנוּ מִיֹּמָיִם בַּיּוֹם הַשְּׁלִישִׁי יְקִמֵנוּ וְנִחְיֶה

לְפָנָיו׃   הושע ה:טו-ו:ב

OLD TESTAMENT SCRIPTURE TRANSLATION

"I will go away *and* return to My place Until they acknowledge their guilt and seek My face; In their affliction they will earnestly seek Me. Come, let us return to the Lord. For He has torn *us*, but He will heal us; He has wounded *us*, but He will bandage us. He will revive us after two days; He will raise us up on the third day That we may live before Him."   **Hosea 5:15-6:2 NASB**

ANCIENT RABBINICAL COMMENTARY

"When King Solomon speaks of his 'beloved,' he usually means Israel the nation. In one instance he compares his beloved to a roe, and therein he refers to a feature which marks alike Moses and the Messiah, the two redeemers of Israel. Just as a roe comes within the range of man's vision only to disappear from sight and then appear again, so it is with these redeemers. Moses appeared to the Israelites, then disappeared, and eventually appeared once more, and the same peculiarity we have in connexion with Messiah; He will appear, disappear, and appear again—Numb. Rabba II. The fourteenth verse in the second chapter of Ruth is thus explained. 'Come thou hither' is the prediction of Messiah's kingdom. 'Dip the morsel in the vinegar,' foretells the agony through which Messiah will pass, as it is written in Isaiah (cap. 53.), 'He was wounded for our sins, He was bruised for our transgressions.' 'And she set herself beside the reapers' predicts the temporary departure of Messiah's kingdom. 'And he reached her parched corn' means the restoration of His kingdom."[22]   **Midrash Ruth 5,**
A Treasury of the Midrash, by Samuel Rapaport, pp. 43-44

NEW TESTAMENT RECORDED 63 AD

"And He said to the disciples, 'The days shall come when you will long to see one of the days of the Son of Man, and you will not see it. And they will say to you, 'Look there! Look here!' Do not go away, and do not run after *them*. For just as the lightning, when it flashes out of one part of the sky, shines to the other part of the sky, so will the Son of Man be in His day. But first He must suffer many things and be rejected by this generation.' "
Jesus (Luke 17:22-25 NASB)

MODERN RABBINIC COMMENT/REFUTATION

"...commentators say that it [Isaiah 53] is speaking of the Prophet Isaiah himself. In any case it cannot be proven that this passage is speaking of the Messiah at all....The main thing is that a clear reading of the Jewish Bible offers absolutely no support to the 'proofs' of Christianity. In most cases, all you need is a good translation (or better still, the Hebrew original), and all those 'proofs' fall away. Many contemporary Christian scholars admit as much. However, the missionaries never mention the most important prophecies concerning the Messiah that Jesus *did not* fulfill. The main task of the Messiah was to bring the world back to G-d, and to abolish all war, suffering and injustice from the world. Clearly, Jesus did not accomplish this. In order to get around this failure on the part of Jesus, Christians invented the doctrine of the 'Second Coming' (Hebrews 9:29, Peter 3). All the prophecies that Jesus did not fulfill the first time are supposed to be taken care of the second time around. However, the Jewish Bible offers absolutely no evidence

---

[22]Samuel Rapaport, *A Treasury of the Midrash*. New York: KTAV Publishing House, Inc., © 1968, pp. 43-44.

to support the Christian doctrine of a 'Second Coming'....All the embarrassing prophecies that he did not fulfill are swept under the rug of a 'Second Coming.' "[23]
The Real Messiah, by Rabbi Aryeh Kaplan, *et al,* **pp. 54-57; 1976**

AUTHOR'S COMMENT—EVANGELICAL CHRISTIAN POSITION
We can assure you that the prophecies of the Second Advent are not "swept under the rug" but are clearly dealt with throughout the New Testament as we will detail in many chapters of this book [vol. I]. The authors[24] of *The Real Messiah* are representative of most of the modern rabbinical attitude toward the Messiahship of Jesus and are guilty of sweeping all of the many prophecies of the Messiah's First Coming, such as Isaiah 53 and Daniel 9:26, under the rabbinical carpet of intolerance and narrow-mindedness. In this book, we document these prophecies as being considered Messianic not only by Christians and Messianic Jews today but also by the most ancient rabbinical commentaries. Hosea, in his explanation of Messiah coming and returning to His place while reviving Israel after two days (2000 years) and living in their literal sight for the third day (1000 years), is speaking of the Messiah. There can be no doubt of this in light of the fact that the Targum Onkelos (ancient rabbinical commentary) identifies this passage with Messiah. This is documented in Alfred Edersheim's book[25], where it says Hosea 6:2 is Messianically applied in the Targum. Jesus will bring war to an end (see my comment on page 37).   **Philip Moore**

THE MESSIAH'S SECOND COMING—COULD IT BE IN OUR GENERATION?

Our answer concerning a date for the Second Coming of the Messiah is the same as Jesus': "...of that day and hour knoweth no *man*...." (Matt. 24:36 KJV).

Our rabbi friends we have quoted, who speculated and made such trivial predictions involving the exact time, should have realized that it was impossible to know even the year. Suffice it to say that it would have done them good to take Jesus' statement seriously—if they had read it, of course.

In our search for the generation of His Advent, we will also examine the words of Jesus which, unlike the rabbis', have yet to be proven in error!

Jesus tells us in the first book of the New Testament: "Now learn a parable of the fig tree [Israel's rebirth].[26] When his branch is yet

---

[23]Aryeh Kaplan *The Real Messiah,* New York, National Conference of Synagogue Youth, 1976, [ ] mine. Rabbi Kaplan's spelling of God as "G-d" is not a typo but the way Orthodox Jews sometimes refer to His name, considering it too holy to write or pronounce outside of a synagogue. In Israel, they say *Elohim* (God) in the synagogue, but *Elokim* outside the synagogue, leaving out the letter *hay*. This is where the written English form, G-d, originated.
[24]This publication is authored by several rabbis writing on various anti-missionary topics.
[25]Alfred Edersheim, *The Life and Times of Jesus the Messiah.* Grand Rapids, MI: Wm B. Eerdmans Publishing Co., © 1971, p. 734.
[26]For conclusive proof that the fig tree is Israel, see our *Israel and the Apocalypse of Newton,* chapter 1, "A Liberal Interpretation on the Prophecy of Israel—Disproved," and

tender, and putteth forth leaves, ye know that summer *is* nigh: So likewise ye, when ye shall see all these things, know that it [the Second Advent of Messiah] is near, *even* at the doors. Verily I say unto you, This generation [the generation which sees Israel become a nation; us!] shall not pass, till all these things [the Second Advent and its accompanying end time events] be fulfilled" (Matt. 24:32-34 KJV; [ ] mine).

We know from Genesis 15:13-16 that a generation can be as long as one hundred years.[27] Since Israel was born in 1948, then according to Jesus, who spoke of Israel's beginning generation, and Moses, who wrote of the maximum length of a generation in Genesis (two prophets who have never been wrong), we should see something before 2048, shouldn't we?

We also have Hosea's calendar in the Old Testament, which speaks of one who had returned to His place after 2000 years, to begin a third 1000-year kingdom (see our *Volume I,* chapter 6, "The Handwriting on the Wall Spelled 'The Temple Falls' ").

Don't get me wrong, we do not believe in setting dates, we are just relying on the limits Jesus set on time parameters drawn on certain events, some of which have already occurred, thus giving us numerical boundaries. Therefore, we suspect that sometime between the year you read this and the era just before the mid-twenty-first century, or shortly thereafter, the ultimate redemption of the planet you and I inhabit, will be brought in by our Messiah Jesus.

During the millennial reign of the Messiah, all of God's creatures will love one another, as was intended in the beginning.

---

our *Nightmare of the Apocalypse,* appendix 3, "Israel—Is Real," an excerpt from our *Vol. I,* chapter 18.

[27]To be even more precise, the children of Israel were in Egypt four hundred and thirty years, which the Bible equates to be four generations in Genesis 15. Thus, if we divided four into four hundred and thirty, we come up with four generations of one hundred seven and one-half years. So a maximum generation of one hundred seven and one-half years, from May 1948, would end in November of 2055, and even sooner if these were three hundred and sixty-day biblical years instead of our three hundred and sixty-five-day solar year. Will we see Jesus before then? This prophetic writer bets his life on it!

ORIGINAL HEBREW TEXT WRITTEN 997 AND 487 BC

כִּי אֶלֶף שָׁנִים בְּעֵינֶיךָ כְּיוֹם אֶתְמוֹל כִּי יַעֲבֹר וְאַשְׁמוּרָה בַלָּיְלָה:

תהלים צ:ד

וְהָיָה יְהוָה לְמֶלֶךְ עַל־כָּל־הָאָרֶץ בַּיּוֹם הַהוּא יִהְיֶה יְהוָה אֶחָד וּשְׁמוֹ אֶחָד:

זכריה יד:ט

OLD TESTAMENT SCRIPTURE TRANSLATION

"For a thousand years in Thy sight Are like yesterday when it passes by, Or *as* a watch in the night." **Psalms 90:4 NASB**

"And the LORD will be king over all the earth; in that day the LORD will be *the only* one and his name *the only* one." **Zechariah 14:9 NASB**

ANCIENT RABBINICAL COMMENTARY

"Another interpretation of 'There was none of them' (Ps. cxxxix. 16) is that it means the seventh day, for this world is to last 6,000 years; 2,000 years....It was waste and desolate; 2,000 years under the Law; 2,000 years under the Messiah. And because our sins are increased, they are prolonged. As they are prolonged, and as we make one day a Sabbatic year, so will God in the latter days make one day a Sabbatic year, which is 1,000 years, and it is said, 'But it shall be one day, which shall be known to the Lord,' this is the seventh day."[28] **Yalkut on Psalm cxxxix. 16**

"For six thousand years the world will exist: [there will be] two thousand years of *Tohu* ['void'], two thousand years of Tora, and two thousand years of the Messiah. But because of our sins, which are many, several of these [Messianic years] have already passed....the Holy One, blessed be He, will renew His world only after seven thousand years."[29] **B. Sanhedrin 97a-b**

"...And the Children of Ishmael [the Arabs] will at that time arise with all the nations of the world to go forth against Jerusalem....Happy will be all those who will remain on the world at the end of the sixth millennium to enter into [the millennium of] the Sabbath...."[30] **Zohar 1:119a**

NEW TESTAMENT RECORDED 96 AD

"Blessed and holy is the one who has a part in the first resurrection; over these the second death has no power, but they will be priests of God and of Christ and will reign with Him for a thousand years." **Revelation 20:6 NASB**

COULD HE RETURN SOONER?

On the other hand, we might see the Messiah return a few years sooner! Nate Krupp, in his book, *The Omega Generation*, points out: "The maximum number of eclipses of the sun and the moon combined that can possibly occur in any single year is seven. Many believe that the year the Balfour Declaration was signed (1917) giving the Jews the right to return to Palestine, ushered in the time of the last generation mentioned by Jesus in Matthew 24:34, also called the time of the

---

[28]Rev. B. Pick, Ph.D., *Old Testament Passages Messianically Applied by the Ancient Synagogue*, published in the compilation *Hebraica, A Quarterly Journal in the Interests of Semitic Study*, Vol. IV, pp. 248-249.
[29]Raphael Patai, *The Messiah Texts*, p. 60.
[30]Ibid, p. 64.

'beginning of sorrows.' In the year 1917 there were seven eclipses of the sun and the moon. As the seventh eclipse appeared, General Allenby marched into Jerusalem, thereby putting into effect the agreements contained within the Balfour Declaration."[31]

We could deductively reason, if this is true and a generation is one hundred years (according to Gen. 15:13-16), that the earliest date for the Coming of Jesus could be 2017 (thus the Rapture[32] would occur in 2010, if this is a correct deduction). No one knows. So we will wait and see with excitement, as Jesus tells us in the New Testament to "look up, and lift up your heads; for your redemption draweth nigh" (Luke 21:28 KJV).

The greatest scientist of all time, Isaac Newton, believed the Jews would return to Jerusalem in the twentieth century and that Jesus would return in the twenty-first century, so we believe Christ's most probable appearance will be between 2017 and 2048. Not long to wait, is it? When you consider that nearly forty half-century increments of time have passed, another fifty years, or less, leaves about one-and-a-half minutes before twelve o'clock midnight, if we are right, in our biblical reasoning.

THE REAL ERA OF THE MESSIAH'S RETURN VERSUS THE FALSE DATES OF PAST RABBIS

The Hebrew prophet Hosea clearly indicated that the Messiah would return two days (2000 years) after He went back to His place, so we only have to ask ourselves, "When did Jesus leave the earth?"

The New Testament, along with recent highly technical scientific calculations, indicates the date of the crucifixion and ascension to have been 33 AD.[33] They were separated by only forty days; thus, if we

---

[31]Nate Krupp, *The Omega Generation*. Harrison, AR: New Leaf Press, Inc., © 1977, p. 137, used by permission.

[32]For those of you unfamiliar with the Rapture, see our *Vol. I*, chapter 25, "The Rapture Factor."

[33]We note that an *Atlanta Journal and Constitution* article mentioned several intriguing points regarding our 33 AD date. The article mentioned that two British scientists, Colin Humphreys and W. G. Waddington, of Oxford University, concluded that Jesus died in April of 33 AD. The British science magazine, *Nature*, reported that they based their conclusions on astronomical, biblical and historical references. The article reported: "The scientists said they were able to reconstruct the Jewish calendar at the time and to date a lunar eclipse which the Bible and other historical sources suggest followed the crucifixion....By a process of elimination they went on to conclude that within the decade from A.D. 26 to A.D. 36, the only possible year for the crucifixion to have occurred was A.D. 33. In the second half of their article, the scientists turn to references in the Bible and in the Apocrypha to the moon's being 'turned to blood,' saying that 'in our view the phrase...probably refers to a lunar eclipse, in which case the crucifixion can be dated unambiguously.' 'The reason an eclipsed moon is blood red is well known,' they wrote. 'Even though the moon is geometrically in the earth's shadow, sunlight still reaches it by refraction in the earth's atmosphere and is reddened by having traversed a long path

subtract thirty-three from 1997 to remind ourselves how long Jesus has been gone, we get 1,964 years. Then to get to the 2000-year period since He left, we must add another thirty-six years to 1997, which would put us into the era of 2033, give or take a few years.[34] This is Hosea's era,[35] not mine! Interestingly enough, Israel's jubilee of the ownership of Jerusalem, recaptured in 1967, will fall on the year 2017! We believe Jesus' return is almost a certainty between 2017 and 2033! The years between 2010 and 2033 will be the most exciting of my life, if Jesus doesn't take me home before then.

Just think, if all the rabbis we mentioned had understood and heeded Hosea's prophecy about the Messiah's Second Coming in light of Jesus' *return to His Father's place*, they would not have guessed the numerous false dates for the Messiah's Coming. They would have done a service to God and themselves. It is because so many have set dates which came and passed, that presently, many doubt the Coming of the Messiah. So much so among many Jewish theologians, that the famous Jewish philosopher, Martin Buber, in his book, *Hasidic Stories Retold,* relates a question put to the Rabbi of Sadagora: "How can this be? A number of holy men who lived before our time alluded to a date on which redemption was to come. The era they indicated has come and gone, but redemption has not come to pass."[36]

In answer to this, the *Tzaddiq* replies: "The light of redemption is spread about us at the level of our heads. We do not notice it because our heads are bowed beneath the burden of exile. Oh, that God might lift up our heads!"[37]

We hope to see the words of Jesus and Hosea fulfilled as prophecies in our day. No doubt, many are, as we see the rapid growth of Jews for Jesus around the globe. In an April 14, 1989, *Jewish Echo*[38] article entitled, "The Numbers of 'Messianic' Jews is Said To Be Growing" by Susan Birnbaum, it was predicted that by the year 2000, the number of Messianic Jews would probably be one-half million. This will be a historic record!

---

through the atmosphere where scattering (of light) preferentially removes the blue end of the spectrum....' " "2 Scientists Determine Exact Crucifixion Date," *Atlanta Journal and Constitution*, Dec. 22, 1983, © reprinted by permission of the Associated Press. Reproduction does not imply endorsement.

[34]This would be even sooner if three hundred and sixty-day biblical years are considered.

[35]Hosea, as he was a prophet of God, speaking and writing the Lord's very own inspired words, cannot be wrong. The many critics of the Second Coming who admit biblical inspiration and inerrancy, few as they may be, may disagree with me, but can they argue with God about His word written through His prophet Hosea? No!

[36]Raphael Patai, *The Messiah Texts*, p. 64.

[37]Ibid, p. 64. Patai's source was *Tales of the Hasidim II: The Later Masters*. New York: A Schocken Book with Farrar, Straus & Young, © 1948. Hasidic stories retold in Buber's style.

[38]Published in Glasgow, Scotland.

IF THE RABBIS WERE MISTAKEN BEFORE, MIGHT THEY ALSO BE WRONG NOW ABOUT JESUS BEING AN IMPOSTER?

Finally, we conclude that since so many rabbis have shamefully been mistaken so many times in the past about the Messiah, could it be that they also erred in failing to recognize who the Messiah was[39] and the expected time of His generation? We believe the Messiah is Jesus and His generation is now.

Jesus gave certain eminent signs, which He said would clearly indicate the nearness of His Coming. He said: "...brother will deliver up brother to death, and a father *his* child; and children will rise up against parents, and cause them to be put to death. And you will be hated by all on account of My name....and A MAN'S ENEMIES WILL BE THE MEMBERS OF HIS HOUSEHOLD....And you will be hearing of wars and rumors of wars; see that you are not frightened, for *those things* must take place, but *that* is not yet the end. For nation will rise against nation, and kingdom against kingdom, and in various places there will be famines [and pestilences] and earthquakes[40]....And because lawlessness is increased, most people's love will grow cold....Therefore when you see the ABOMINATION OF DESOLATION which was spoken of through Daniel the prophet, standing in the holy place (let the reader understand), then let those who are in Judea flee to the mountains[41]....there will be a great tribulation...." (Matt. 10:21-22, 36; 24:6-12, 15-16, 21 NASB; [ ] mine, KJV insertion).

---

[39] It is also interesting to note that Rabbis and Jewish leaders have misguessed and been mistaken about the identity of the Messiah all through history! Virtually every era has witnessed a false Jewish Messiah. To mention a few: Menachem–first century; Bar Cochba–second century; Moses of Crete–fifth century; Abu Isa–eighth century; David Alroy–twelfth century; Abraham Abulafia–1240-1291; Abraham ben Samuel–circa 1300; Moses Botarel–fourteenth century; Asher Lammlein–1502; David Reuveni–sixteenth century; Hayyim Vital–1574; Solomon Molko–sixteenth century; Sabbatai Zevi–1626-1676; Berehiah–1700s; Jacob Frank–eighteenth century; and Ari Shocher–nineteenth century.

[40]Concerning Jesus' end time sign of earthquakes, Zionist evangelist television preacher, John Hagee, documented at the end of 1993: "In the 15th century there were 115 earthquakes; in the 16th there were 253; in the 17th there were 378; in the 18th century there were 640; in the 19th century there were 2119; in the 20th century we've had so many earthquakes so fast we can hardly keep records of them. We have a department now trying to predict where the next big one is going to take place...." John Hagee, *Israel and the PLO Peace Pact: Hope or Hoax, Evidence of the Last Generation on Earth.* See our *Nightmare of the Apocalypse,* appendix 4, "Earthquakes," for an expert seismologist's documentations on "World Earthquakes and Seismicity Rates".

[41]See our *Nightmare of the Apocalypse,* Appendix 9, "They Escaped to Petra."

ORIGINAL HEBREW TEXT WRITTEN 712 BC

הַעִירֹותִי מִצָּפֹון וַיֵּאת מִמִּזְרַח־שֶׁמֶשׁ יִקְרָא בִשְׁמִי וְיָבֹא סְגָנִים כְּמֹו־חֹמֶר וּכְמֹו יֹצֵר יִרְמָס־

טִיט: .... הָאֹמֵר לַצּוּלָה חֲרָבִי וְנַהֲרֹתַיִךְ אֹובִישׁ:

ישעיה מא:כה; מד:כז

OLD TESTAMENT SCRIPTURE TRANSLATION

"...he has come; From the rising of the sun....*It is I* who says to the depth of the sea, 'Be dried up!' And I will make your rivers dry."

Isaiah 41:25; 44:27 NASB

ANCIENT RABBINICAL COMMENTARY

"And again the spirit carried me and took me to the east of the world, and I saw there stars battling one another and resting not."[42]

Sefer Eliyahu, BhM 3:65-67

"...the kings of the East will congregate....They will offer sacrifices in Jerusalem....The kings of the East will say, 'He is giving the Israelites permission to build the house of the sanctuary,' and they will come to burn it. Then the holy One blessed be He will go out and fight with them, to fulfill that which is said, *The Lord will go out and fight with those Gentiles* (Zech 14:3)."[43]

Midrash Suta Hagadische Abhandlungen uber
Schir haSchirim, Ruth, Eikah, und Koheleth

"...Gog and Magog will come against Israel, he and all the kings of the East...."[44]

The Book of Zerubbabel, text of Pirke Hecalot Rabbati

NEW TESTAMENT RECORDED 96 AD

"And the number of the armies of the horsemen was two hundred million; I heard the number of them....And the sixth *angel* poured out his bowl upon the great river, the Euphrates; and its water was dried up, that the way might be prepared for the kings from the east....And they gathered them together to the place which in Hebrew is called HarMagedon." **Revelation 9:16; 16:12, 16 NASB**

MODERN RABBINIC COMMENT/REFUTATION

"Jews....believe that man will not self-destruct, that we will not disappear in a gigantic atomic blast. Man is basically good...."

The Real Messiah, by Aryeh Kaplan, *et al,* p. 50; 1976

MODERN POLITICAL COMMENT

"Political power comes out of the barrel of a gun. The gun must never slip from the grasp of the Chinese communist party." "Israel...[is] 'the Formosa [free China] of the Mediterranean' which should be swept into the sea."[45]

Mao Tse-tung, Communist China's first Premier; 1949

"As China marches southwestward, China is grabbing all the deep water ports in the China Sea and expanding its exploration for oil. We believe that the 'Mid-East' is a prime target and oil is the magnet that is drawing China Southwestward. The

---

[42]Raphael Patai, *The Messiah Texts*, p. 150.

[43]George W. Buchanan, *Revelation and Redemption*, Dillsboro, NC: Western North Carolina Press, © 1978, p. 449, used by permission.

[44]Ibid, p. 345.

[45]Karl Marx, *A World Without Jews*, New York, Philosophical Library Inc., © 1959 (Introduction by Dagobert Runes) p. viii. [ ] mine. In case you don't know, Formosa is the last vestige of freedom left in China. It is a small unconquered island located off the coast of China, still a democracy as of mid-1997, known to the world as Taiwan. Is there any hint at why China continues to openly and secretly train PLO terrorists?

sleeping giant is awakening and the Far/Mid-East will become more dangerous in the coming years!"[46]   **"Taipan;" 1995**

AUTHOR'S COMMENT—EVANGELICAL CHRISTIAN POSITION

For some time now, we have possessed the A-bomb and China is still claiming, as she has since the 1970's, that she can field a People's Army of 200,000,000 soldiers, the exact number John mentioned in Revelation 16, 2000 years ago when there were not that many people on the entire planet.   What will the 2020's to 2030's reveal regarding war?   We believe plenty?   It is quite clear that many modern rabbis' conception of a permanent peace, formulated and enforced with no nuclear confrontation, is in error, as far as the Bible verses and rabbinical writings we have quoted are concerned.   There will be peace, but lasting peace will only come when Jesus is received by His people.   Only the Messiah can bring peace upon His acceptance, and this, as the Bible teaches, will only occur when He saves the world from Armageddon!   **Philip Moore**

An illustration of the Second Coming, as predicted in the Scriptures.

---

[46]"International Intelligence Briefing," Feb. 1995. Palos Verdes, CA: Hal Lindsey Ministries, p. 6. Available through HLM, 1-800-TITUS-35.

The Jewish prophet Zechariah, twenty-five hundred years in retrospect, tells us the Messiah (Jesus) will return to the Mount of Olives in Jerusalem, Israel. "For I will gather all nations against Jerusalem to battle; and the city shall be taken, and the houses rifled, and the women ravished; and half of the city shall go forth into captivity, and the residue of the people shall not be cut off from the city. Then shall the LORD go forth, and fight against those nations, as when he fought in the day of battle. And his feet shall stand in that day upon the mount of Olives, which *is* before Jerusalem on the east, and the mount of Olives shall cleave in the midst thereof toward the east and toward the west, *and there shall be* a very great valley; and half of the mountain shall remove toward the north, and half of it toward the south. And ye shall flee *to* the valley of the mountains; for the valley of the mountains shall reach unto Azal: yea, ye shall flee, like as ye fled from before the earthquake in the days of Uzziah king of Judah: and **the LORD my God shall come**, *and* all the saints with thee" (Zech 14:2-5 KJV; bold mine).

Zechariah also predicted, in God's very words, "And it shall come to pass in that day, *that* I will seek to destroy all the nations that come against Jerusalem. And I will pour upon the house of David, and upon the inhabitants of Jerusalem, the spirit of grace and of supplications: and they shall look upon **me** whom they **have pierced**, and they shall mourn for him, as one mourneth for *his* only *son*, and shall be in bitterness for him, as one that is in bitterness for *his* firstborn. In that day shall there be a great mourning in Jerusalem, as the mourning of Hadadrimmon in the valley of Megiddon. And the land shall mourn, every family apart; the family of the house of David apart, and their wives apart; the family of the house of Nathan apart, and their wives apart; The family of the house of Levi apart, and their wives apart; the family of Shimei apart, and their wives apart; All the families that remain, every family apart, and their wives apart" (Zech. 12:9-14 KJV, bold mine).

The New Testament (covenant) tells us: "Behold, he cometh with clouds; and every eye shall see him, and they *also* which pierced him: and all kindreds of the earth shall wail because of him. Even so, Amen" (Rev. 1:7 KJV; 96 AD). Jesus Himself vowed to the High Priests of His day, while He was under oath, "... nevertheless, I tell you, hereafter you shall see the son of man [Messiah, i.e., Himself] sitting at the right hand of power [God Almighty], and coming on the clouds of heaven" (Matt. 26:64 NASB, [ ] mine). These conditions were foretold regarding the Messiah for the last days in Psalm 110:1[47] and Daniel. Over 2500 years ago, Daniel predicted: "I saw in the night

---

[47] See Dr. David Flussers comment on this Psalm and Jesus on page 19 of the author's latest book, *Nightmare of the Apocalypse: The Rabbi Conspiracy.*

visions, and behold, one like the Son of man came with the clouds of heaven, and came to the Ancient of days, and they brought him near before him. And there was given him dominion, and glory, and a kingdom, that all people, nations, and languages should serve him: his dominion is an everlasting dominion, which shall not pass away, and his kingdom that which shall not be destroyed" (Daniel 7:13, 14 KJV). We believe Jesus will return in this way to the Mount of Olives in our generation!

The Mount of Olives, where Jesus stood, before ascending into the heavens, and to which He will soon return (Acts 1:10, 11)!

This face of the Mount of Olives is covered with thousands of Jewish tombstones placed there by the Orthodox because they expect the Messiah will come here first just before He redeems the entire Earth due to Zechariah's above prophetical writings.

ORIGINAL HEBREW TEXT WRITTEN 487 BC

וְזֹאת ׀ תִּהְיֶה הַמַּגֵּפָה אֲשֶׁר יִגֹּף יְהוָה אֶת־כָּל־הָעַמִּים אֲשֶׁר צָבְאוּ עַל־יְרוּשָׁלָ͏ִם הָמֵק ׀ בְּשָׂרוֹ וְהוּא עֹמֵד עַל־רַגְלָיו וְעֵינָיו תִּמַּקְנָה בְחֹרֵיהֶן וּלְשׁוֹנוֹ תִּמַּק בְּפִיהֶם: וְהָיָה בַּיּוֹם הַהוּא תִּהְיֶה מְהוּמַת־יְהוָה רַבָּה בָּהֶם וְהֶחֱזִיקוּ אִישׁ יַד רֵעֵהוּ וְעָלְתָה יָדוֹ עַל־יַד רֵעֵהוּ׃ וְגַם־יְהוּדָה תִּלָּחֵם בִּירוּשָׁלָ͏ִם וְאֻסַּף חֵיל כָּל־הַגּוֹיִם סָבִיב זָהָב וָכֶסֶף וּבְגָדִים לָרֹב מְאֹד׃

זכריה יד:יב-יד

OLD TESTAMENT SCRIPTURE TRANSLATION

"Now this will be the plague with which the LORD will strike all the peoples who have gone to war against Jerusalem; their **flesh** will rot while they stand on their feet, and their eyes will rot in their sockets, and their tongue will rot in their mouth. And it will come about in that day that a great panic from the LORD will fall on them; and they will seize one another's hand, and the hand of one will be lifted against the hand of another. And Judah also will fight at Jerusalem...."

Zechariah 14:12-14 NASB

ANCIENT RABBINICAL COMMENTARY

"And what did Gog think? He said: 'Pharaoh who went forth against Israel was a fool, for he let their Patron [i.e., God] be and went against them, and likewise Amalek and Sisera, and all those who arose against them. They let the Holy One, blessed be He, be; they were fools. But I, what will I do? I shall go forth first against the Patron of Israel, [since] if I first slay the Messiah, he will cause other Messiahs to arise. Therefore I shall go against the Holy One, blessed be He....' What did they [the hosts of Gog] do? They stood on their feet and looked up toward the Holy One, blessed be He, and said: *'Come, let us cut them off from being a nation, that the name of Israel may be no more in remembrance* (Ps. 83:5).' What does 'the Name of Israel' mean? They said: 'Let us uproot Him who wrote, *Blessed be the Lord, the God of Israel* (Ps. 41:14).' And what does the Holy One, blessed be He, do to them from Above? They stand on their feet, and He punishes them....[He says:] 'Those feet which wanted to stand up against Me, *Their flesh shall consume away while they stand upon their feet* (Zech. 14:12). And those eyes which looked up, *And their eyes shall consume away in their sockets* (ibid.). And that tongue which spoke against the Lord, *And their tongue shall consume away in their mouth* (ibid.).' The Holy One, blessed be He, says to them: 'At first you were not at peace with one another....And now you made peace with one another so as to come against Me....I, too, shall do likewise. I shall call the birds and the beasts who were not at peace with one another, and I shall cause them to be at peace with one another in order to go forth against you. And because you said, *That the name of Israel may be no more in remembrance* (Ps. 83:5), by your life, you will die and they will bury you and will take a name [i.e., become famous] in the world.' "[48]

Aggadat B'reshit, ed. Buber, pp. 5-7

"The tradition may have even anticipated the tremendous destructive powers of our modern technology. Thus, we have the teaching of Rabbi Elazar that the Messianic Age will begin in a generation with the power to destroy itself."[49]

Rabbi Elazar of the first century

NEW TESTAMENT RECORDED 37AD

"...'Take heed that no man deceive you....And ye shall hear of wars and rumours of wars: see that ye be not troubled: for all *these things* must come to pass, but the end is not yet. For nation shall rise against nation, and kingdom against kingdom: and there shall be famines, and pestilences, and earthquakes, in divers places....ye

---

[48]Raphael Patai, *The Messiah Texts*, pp. 149-150. Bold mine.

[49]Rabbi Aryeh Kaplan, *et al*, *The Real Messiah*, p. 67.

shall be hated of all nations for my name's sake....many false prophets shall rise, and shall deceive many....When ye therefore shall see the abomination of desolation, spoken of by Daniel the prophet, stand in the holy place, (whoso readeth, let him understand:) Then let them which be in Judæa flee into the mountains....then shall be great tribulation, such as was not since the beginning of the world to this time, no, nor ever shall be. And except those days should be shortened, there should no **flesh** be saved: but for the elect's sake those days shall be shortened....Behold, I have told you before.' "

Matthew 24:4, 6-7, 9, 11, 15-16, 21-22, 25 KJV

MODERN RABBINIC COMMENT/REFUTATION

"There are some pessimists who say that mankind is approaching its end. They predict that we will either pollute ourselves off the face of this planet or overpopulate to the barest marginal existence. Others see man doing the job more quickly, bringing his civilization crashing down on his head in a nuclear war."

The Real Messiah, **by Rabbi Aryeh Kaplan, *et al*, p. 63; 1976**

MODERN POLITICAL SCIENTIFIC FACT

"We have had our last chance. If we will not devise some greater and more equitable system, ARMAGEDDON will be at the door. The problem basically is theological and involves a spiritual recrudescence and improvement of human character that will synchronize with our almost matchless advances in science, art, literature, and all material and cultural developments of the past 2000 years. It must be the spirit if we are to save the flesh."

General Douglas MacArthur, at Japanese surrender; 1945

"There is no defense[50] in science against the weapons which can now destroy civilization." [51]   **Albert Einstein; 1955**

"If the Israelis threaten us, we will wipe them out within two days. I can assure you our plans are made for this eventuality."[52]

Soviet Ambassador Anatoly Dobrynin; 1972

"You know, I turn back to your ancient prophets in the Old Testament and the signs foretelling Armageddon, and I find myself wondering if—if we're the generation that is going to see that come about. I don't know if you've noted any of those prophecies lately, but, believe me, they certainly describe the times."[53] "We see around us today the marks of a terrible dilemma, predictions of doomsday. Those predictions carry weight because of the existence of nuclear weapons, and the

---

[50]It is interesting that just as we were developing a defense (President Reagan's Star Wars nuclear defense shield), in late 1993, President Clinton cancelled this would-be life-saving project, further validating Einstein's statement. We pray that we soon elect a responsible president who will invest in the protection of this nation's families, hopefully redeploying this scientific, Strategic Defence Initiative (and the latest in defense technology) before it is too late. For the Bible does not state whether anyone will or will not escape annihilation; apparently God is leaving this up to us. Though we know some areas of the world will suffer, the Bible does not mention the U.S. or its number of casualties!

[51]Hal Lindsey with C.C. Carlson, *The Late Great Planet Earth*. Grand Rapids: Zondervan Publishing House, © 1970, p. 146.

[52]Mike Evans, *The Return*. New York: Thomas Nelson Publishers, © 1986, p. 184.

[53]"Reagan: Is Apocalypse Now?" *Atlanta Journal and Constitution*, Sat., Oct. 29, 1983, reprinted by permission of Associated Press. Reproduction does not imply endorsement.

constant threat of global war...so much so that no president, no congress, no parliament can spend a day entirely free of this threat."[54]
President Ronald Reagan; 1983
"A nuclear confrontation in the Middle East is not just likely, it is certain. It is just a matter of timing."   **Robert Hunter,**
US Ambassador to NATO; 1996

AUTHOR'S COMMENT—EVANGELICAL CHRISTIAN POSITION
In light of the Old Testament biblical prophet Zechariah's awesome description of end time war, which could only be nuclear, coupled with Rabbi Elazar's point that the Messianic age would only begin in a generation with the power to destroy itself, we see interesting illumination in Albert Einstein's comment, as stated above, and in those who politically threaten the security of Israel and the West today. Thus, Jesus' words of warning about the war in the last days and His advice to the Jews to flee to the mountains until His return, in the space of the future seven-year tribulation period[55] take on an immense importance. All of this undermines Rabbi Kaplan's irresponsible statement in *The Real Messiah*, to the effect that we will graduate into a Messianic peace without the war predicted by Jesus. Had Rabbi Kaplan read the commentaries of his own Jewish predecessors, he would have been more informed in this matter. If Mr. Kaplan were alive today, I would love to discuss these commentaries with him. Shouldn't we all heed the words of the Bible and New Testament as they become more evident in the end time scenario presently developing? Yes!   **Philip Moore**

IF ALL THIS IS TRUE ABOUT *YESHUA* (JESUS)—IF HE IS THE MESSIAH—WHAT DO I DO NOW?

After considering the incredible prophecies you have read, if you have not received God's love gift of forgiveness, which Messiah purchased by taking the judgement of God that was due our short comings, then we can take care of it now, as we read and ponder the truth of the Scriptures. We do not have to understand every detail or have a "perfect" faith, all we need to realize is that God offers us an across the board pardon and new life in the Messiah *Yeshua*, Jesus.

Jesus tells us that we may receive His atonement for us by inviting Him, in a simple way, into our hearts (Rev. 3:20). Just thank the Messiah for giving His life for you, as was described by the Jewish prophet Isaiah, in the fifty-third chapter of his predictions you read earlier. Tell *Yeshua* now, "Come in—thank you!" It is like His Father, God, is a civil judge, who would like to let us go for whatever crime we have committed, but cannot because we do not have the money to pay our own required fine.

His son loves us so that He stands up in the courtroom and says: "Wait Dad, I've got the money to pay for his violation—his penalty!" The judge (God) says, "My son wants to pay for you. If you accept His payment, then I am able to let you go free—forever—so take it,

---

[54]Mike Evans, *The Return*, p. 94.
[55]See "They Escaped to Petra" in the author's *Nightmare of the Apocalypse* for details.

and run with it! He loves you!" Now that you have received Him, the Messiah promises: "I will never desert you, nor will I ever forsake you" (Heb. 13:5 NASB).

Every time you blunder, confess (agree that it was not proper in God's ideal will, then tell God *Yeshua* paid for it; I John 1:9 instructs that a believer is continually cleansed and brought into fellowship this way). Then ask Him to fill you anew with power through His spirit. He will do this—even if you ask him forty times[56] a day—that will keep you in direct fellowship with God and will allow you to live free of guilt, as He took our guilt!

If He paid with His life in the horrible way that He did, we have no reason to believe that His death was not enough! We can be sure and **know** with certainty that we will inherit paradise forever in the Messiah's coming kingdom and enjoy life to its fullest now, with a new sense of power, purpose and meaning, for the next few years that we live. However long that may be, five or fifty-five years are nothing compared to eternity, and if we should die before He returns, we will be with Him (I Cor. 5:3), and when He comes He will resurrect our bodies (John 5:28-29) and we will possess new bodies like His own (Phil. 3:21), which will even be able to pass through physical objects (John 20:19, 26)! That is forever—forever is forever—in paradise for the believer! Hope to see you soon in the kingdom. Love you, Shalom! שלום

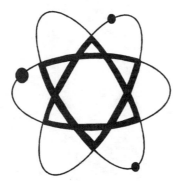

This beautiful molecular symbol reminds us of God's three-dimensional nature, the triangle, with its three sides pointed downward, represents God (Father, Messiah and Spirit; Isa. 48:16) and three-dimensional make up of man (mind, body and spirit; I Thes. 5:23). Looking upward toward God, of which the Messiah was both! The Star of David, formed by the union of the two, fits the atomic symbol

---

[56]Jesus said, in reference to a brother's misconduct toward us, to forgive "seventy times seven" (Matt. 18:21-22 KJV). How much more then will God forgive us when we come to Him in Jesus' name? Much more!

and reminds us of the verse: "And he is before all things, and by him all things consist" (Col. 1:17 KJV). Even one of the smallest representation of matter seems to be symbolically included here.

Lastly, we emphasize that if you happen to be a Jew and are pondering receiving Jesus as your personal Messiah, Savior and Passover[57] sacrifice (I Cor. 5:7-8), there will be some who will try to tell you, "you will not be Jewish anymore," to frighten you from the faith.[58] Of course we can understand their fear and insecurity about a belief they may not have researched or become familiar with, however, nothing could be further from the truth. If you are Jewish how could you become less Jewish by believing in the Jewish Messiah and what He did for you? You cannot! In your new faith, you will become a better Jew—a Messianic Jew!

Sherry Sussman (right), a Messianic Jew in Israel,
celebrates Hanukkah with her friend in Jerusalem.[59]

---

[57]See our publication, *Nightmare of the Apocalypse: The Rabbi Conspiracy,* appendix 6, "The Secrets of Jesus in Passover Versus the Errors of Easter," an excerpt from *Vol. II.*

[58]See our publication, *Nightmare of the Apocalypse: the Rabbi Conspiracy,* appendix 7, "The Real Jewish Bible Ends in Revelation," an excerpt from *Vol. II.*

[59]If you are Jewish and would like to attend a Messianic congregation, see our directory, *Messianic Synagogues: How to Get There,* which is at the end of the author's *Nightmare of the Apocalypse* or call Jews for Jesus at 415-864-2600 to locate your neighborhood Messianic congregation.

"For if it had not been for the Christians, our remnant would surely have been destroyed, and Israel's hope would have been extinguished amidst the Gentiles, who hate us because of our faith....But God, our Lord, has caused the Christian wise men to arise, who protect us in every generation."[1]   Rabbi Emden, 1757

"...[true] Christianity...distinguished itself, in the particular of rescuing Jewish children, by the highest degree of self-sacrifice. It may be stated without exaggeration that almost the entire remnant of Israel which was found in the liberated countries—no matter how small its number—has the Christians to thank for its preservation, Christians who, by performing this action, placed their own lives in danger."[2]   Sholem Asch, Jewish scholar and author, 1945

"It's not possible for a man to say, 'I'm a Christian,' and not love the Jewish people. You cannot be a Christian without being Jewish in spirit."[3] Rev. John Hagee, 1980

"Your [Christian] sympathy, solidarity and belief in the future of Israel—this to us is tremendous. We consider you part of the fulfillment of the prophetic vision expressed by Zechariah in Chapter 14. Your presence here will always remain a golden page in the book of eternity in heaven. May the Lord bless you out of Zion."[4]   Chief Rabbi of Jerusalem, Shlomo Goren, 1980

"The evangelical community is the largest and fastest growing block of pro-Israeli, pro-Jewish sentiment in this country."[5]
     The late Rabbi Marc Tannenbaum, the American-Jewish Committee's national interreligious affairs director, 1981

"One of the great questions in the world is 'Who is a Jew?' An equally great question is 'Who is a Christian?' Millions who profess Christianity could not possibly be true Christians in the biblical sense. For example, if a professing Christian is not dominated by love of neighbor, then he or she cannot possibly be called Christian. Thus many of the persecutions of history were caused by false Christians....I am an evangelical Christian who believes that God can be experienced in daily life and that we are known not only by the creeds we repeat but by the love we live out in our relations with our fellow men and women. Evangelical Christians especially have an affinity for the Jews because the Bible they love is essentially a Jewish book...."[6]   World-renowned evangelist, Dr. Billy Graham, 1985

APPENDIX 3
MEANWHILE, TRUE BELIEVERS IN JESUS LOVE ISRAEL TO THE END

This appendix is pictorial and is meant to illustrate that presently, and in the future, before the Messiah Jesus returns, true evangelical Christians vow to stand by Israel as they did the Jews during the holocaust.[7] Enjoy!

---

[1]Pinchas Lapide, *Israelis, Jews, and Jesus*, New York: Doubleday & Company, Inc., 1979, p. 105. Lapide's source was *Lechem Shamayim* (Hamburg, 1757), p. 30 ff.

[2]Sholem Asch, *One Destiny*, New York: Putnam's © 1945, p. 77, [ ] mine.

[3]Rev. John Hagee, *Why We Honor the Jews*. This audio tape is available through John Hagee Ministries, POB 1400, San Antonio, TX, USA 78295.

[4]"The Press of Israel on the International Christian Embassy Jerusalem," Jerusalem: International Christian Embassy, [ ] mine.

[5]The *Washington Post*, Mar. 23, 1981.

[6]Leonard C. Yaseen, *The Jesus Connection, To Triumph Over Anti-Semitism*. New York: The Crossroad Publishing Company, © 1985, p. ix, used by permission.

[7] The Holocaust was prophesized by Moses and warned of by Jesus. See our Volume I, Chapters 12-14, 18.

Jerusalem Post coverage of the Second International Christian Zionist Congress by Melanie Rosenberg, shows Israel's interest in Christian Zionism, reproduction courtesy of the *Jerusalem Post*.

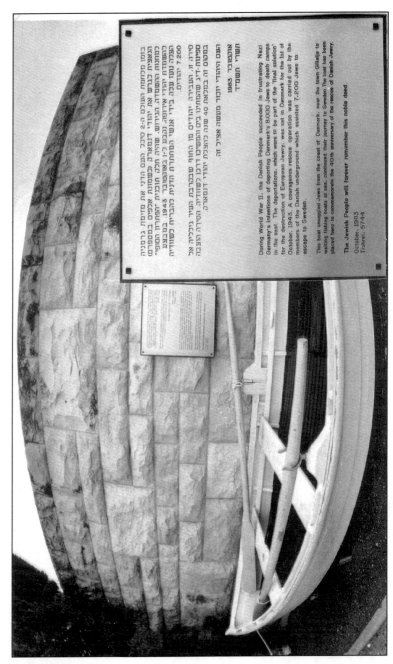

This small boat was used by the Danes to smuggle Jews from Gillelje, Denmark, to fishing boats at sea, on their way to the safety of Sweden.

Here are a few books written by Jewish survivors of the Holocaust. They say they owe their lives to those Christians who aided them in their fight for suvival and Jesus, the one they came to realize is the Jewish Messiah, through whom they were miraculously preserved.

This citation is presented by Yad VaShem to righteous Gentiles in honor of their commitment to save Jews during the Nazi Holocaust.

The entrance to the Garden of the Righteous Gentiles, which leads to the Yad VaShem Holocaust Museum in Jerusalem. The garden is filled with plaques and trees, to honor those Christians who saved Jews, at risk of their own lives from the Nazis.

Corrie Ten Boom, the loving old woman whose book, *The Hiding Place*, later became a film,[8] saved many Jews in her own personal "hiding place" behind a double wall in her home. Corrie was a wonderful Evangelical Christian who said she was willing to save Jesus' people, the Jews, from the Holocaust even if it meant her death. Even though she was relentlessly beaten by the Gestapo, she never turned in any of the Jews she was hiding. Recently, Corrie died and her tree was placed in the Yad VaShem Memorial Park in Israel.

Corrie Ten Boom's name plaque and tree.

The famous Christian Swedish diplomat, Raul Wallenberg, who some feel is still alive and incarcerated in Russia, saved 100,000 Jews. Dr. Arieh L. Bauminger describes this "angel of mercy":[9] "...Wallenberg rented 32 houses that he proclaimed a Swedish extraterritorial zone. Into these houses Wallenberg brought his 'protected Jews,' after having duly provided them with forged papers in the name of the Swedish Embassy and the Red Cross."[10]

Bauminger went on to tell how Wallenberg hid the Jewish children in "churches or private Christian homes," and that: " 'All this was done by a courageous man who had the strength of his convictions to act according to his conscience and beliefs. As in the case of King Christian of Denmark, Wallenberg's deeds once more bring to mind the poignant thought: how much greater could have been the number of survivors in the lands of extermination, had there been others like him....' "[11]

---

[8]This film is now available on home video.

[9]Bauminger, Arieh L. *The Righteous*, Third Edition. Jerusalem: Yad VaShem Martyrs and Heroes Remembrance Authority, © 1983, p. 79, used by permission.

[10]Ibid.

[11]Ibid, p. 81. Attorney General of Israel at the Eichmann trial.

The Wallenberg Memorial, in Jerusalem, built to honor the man
who saved 100,000 Jews from the Holocaust.

OTHER BOOKS BY THE SAME AUTHOR

The End of History—Messiah Conspiracy, Volume I, is over 1,200 pages and contains more than 600 illustrations and photos! *The End of History—Messiah Conspiracy*, Volume I, also features the following chapters and appendices:

To order, please contact:

The Conspiracy, Incorporated
P. O. Box 12227, Atlanta, GA, USA 30355
Toll Free: 1-800-RAMS HEAD (1-800-726-7432)
E-Mail: theconinc@aol.com
Fax: 404-816-9994

You may also obtain this book through your local bookstore by requesting *The End of History—Messiah Conspiracy*, by Philip N. Moore.

Titles available from The Conspiracy, Incorporated, by Philip Moore:

The End of History—Messiah Conspiracy, **Volume I**, contains incredible evidence of the greatest conspiracy of all time—The Messiah Conspiracy, whereby the rabbis of early time sought to cover up the prophecies of their own Bible, indicating Jesus was the Messiah. The motives behind this are both fascinating and shocking. In the little-known town of Yavne, a curse was devised to separate Jewish believers in Jesus from the Jews who had not yet believed—it was called the *Birkat ha-Minim*. We reproduce a recently discovered fragment of this document in Hebrew, which mentions Jewish Christians (*Nazarenes*) beside the word *minim*, which indicates Jewish sects. (1,238 pg.; $29.00 plus shipping and handling)

The End of History—Messiah Conspiracy, Volume I Abridged, contains much of the above but is a smaller book for those who read less, but are eager to give this work as gifts to unsaved friends in greater numbers. (Due out in 1998; approx480 pg.; $19.00 plus shipping and handling)

Israel and the Apocalypse of Newton, (excerpts from *The End of History—Messiah Conspiracy Volume I & II—Essays*). Contains the excerpt *A Liberal Interpretation on the Prophecy of Israel—Disproved*. A short treatise, which quotes Hal Lindsey, M.R. DeHaan, M.D., Reverend Clarence Larkin, Gedaliah Alon, *The Apocalypse of Peter*, and, of course, Jesus Himself, all of whom provide evidence that the liberal "Christian" attack, which continues to claim that modern Israel is not the fulfillment of Bible prophecy, is in error! Gary DeMar and David Chilton, of the "Christian" Reform Movement (CRM), who also hold this view, are thoroughly refuted, as we demonstrate from the Scriptures, that their claim cannot possibly stand. It is our firm belief that the CRM, with their dangerous doctrines of deceit, is an anti-Semitic movement, and should be exposed by true Christians for the falsehoods it teaches, preaches and propagates (in relation to our Evangelical interpretation of the Scriptures) among the laymen of today. Contains chapters 11-16, 19, 26-27, 29-30 of Volume I. (380 pg.)

Nightmare of the Apocalypse (excerpts from *The End of History—Messiah Conspiracy Volume II—Essays*). (350 pg.)

ORDER FORM

Please Print
Name _____
Address _____
City_____ State ____ Zip _____ Phone _____

Quantity	Code	Description	Price	Total
	Book 1	The End of History—Messiah Conspiracy, Volume I	$29.00	
	Book 2	The End of History—Messiah Conspiracy, Volume I Abridged	$19.00	
	Book 3	Israel and the Apocalypse of Newton	$17.00	
	Book 4	Nightmare of the Apocalypse—The Rabbi Conspiracy	$15.00	
	Book 5	Eternal Security for True Believers	$5.00	
	Tapes	Testimony Tapes of Israeli Messianic Believers	$3.00	
	Video	Garden Tomb Tour Video	$17.00	
		One low shipping and handling fee (per order)	$4.95	$4.95
			Total	

Mail along with your check or money order to:
The Conspiracy, Inc., P.O. Box 12227, Atlanta, Georgia, USA, 30355

Zerox this form and order your new book today!

VOL. I CONTAINS OVER 50 PAGES OF COMPARISONS LIKE THESE:

ORIGINAL HEBREW TEXT WRITTEN 710 BC

וְאַתָּה בֵּית־לֶחֶם אֶפְרָתָה צָעִיר לִהְיוֹת בְּאַלְפֵי יְהוּדָה מִמְּךָ לִי יֵצֵא לִהְיוֹת מוֹשֵׁל בְּיִשְׂרָאֵל
וּמוֹצָאֹתָיו מִקֶּדֶם מִימֵי עוֹלָם: מיכה ה:א

OLD TESTAMENT SCRIPTURE TRANSLATION

"But as for you, Bethlehem Ephrathah, *Too* little to be among the clans of Judah, From you One will go forth for Me to be ruler in Israel. His goings forth are from long ago, From the days of eternity." **Micah 5:2 NASB**

ANCIENT RABBINICAL COMMENTARY

"And you, O Bethlehem Ephrath, you who were too small to be numbered among the thousands of the house of Judah, from you shall come forth before Me the Messiah, to exercise dominion over Israel, he whose name was mentioned from before, from the days of creation."[1]   **Targum Jonathan**

" 'Son of Judah, Judaean! Tie your ox and tie your plow, for the King Messiah has been born!'....He asked him: 'From where is he?' He answered: 'From the royal fort of Bethlehem in Judah.' "[2] *Jerusalem Talmud, Berachoth, fol. 5a*

NEW TESTAMENT RECORDED 63 AD

"Now it came about in those days that a decree went out from Caesar Augustus, that a census be taken of all the inhabited earth. This was the first census taken while Quirinius was governor of Syria. And all were proceeding to register for the census, everyone to his own city. And Joseph also went up from Galilee, from the city of Nazareth, to Judea, to the city of David, which is called Bethlehem, because he was of the house and family of David, in order to register, along with Mary, who was engaged to him, and was with child. And it came about that while they were there, the days were completed for her to give birth. And she gave birth to her first-born son; and she wrapped Him in cloths, and laid Him in a manger, because there was no room for them in the inn." **Luke 2:1-7 NASB**

MODERN RABBINIC COMMENT/REFUTATION

"...there is one more verse on the divinity of the Messiah which serves double duty by demonstrating his birth in Bethlehem as well. (Micah 5:1 = 5:2 in some translations). The Christological translation of the last phrase (*miqedem mimei 'olam*) is 'of old, from everlasting,' which demonstrates that this ruler is eternal and hence divine. But aside from the almost immediate reference to 'the Lord his God,' we are once again dealing with a mistranslation...according to the most probable reading of this verse, it not only fails to say that the Messiah is everlasting, it doesn't even say that he will be born in Bethlehem."
Jews and "Jewish Christianity," by David Berger and
Michael Wyschograd, pp. 44-45; © 1978

AUTHOR'S COMMENT—EVANGELICAL CHRISTIAN POSITION

With all due respect, this verse certainly does indicate that the Messiah would be born in Bethlehem and be eternal. Many times this author has shown the Hebrew of Micah 5 to Jews in Israel. They would smile and say, "What an interesting verse. It is so specific about His birthplace, and yet, it shows that He is from forever, as you say." Also, the Jerusalem Talmud and Targum Jonathan, two major Jewish commentaries, say this verse refers to Bethlehem as the birthplace of the Messiah. Hoping not to offend, we suggest David Berger, and the other authors and rabbis of the anti-missionary writings we have quoted in this book, brush up on their Hebrew and ancient rabbinical commentary. **Philip Moore**

---

[1]Samson H. Levey, *The Messiah: An Aramaic Interpretation, The Messianic Exegesis of the Targum*, p. 93.
[2]Raphael Patai, *The Messiah Texts*, p. 123.

ORIGINAL HEBREW TEXT WRITTEN 487 BC

בַּיּוֹם הַהוּא יָגֵן יְהוָה בְּעַד יוֹשֵׁב יְרוּשָׁלַם וְהָיָה הַנִּכְשָׁל בָּהֶם בַּיּוֹם הַהוּא כְּדָוִיד וּבֵית דָּוִיד
כֵּאלֹהִים כְּמַלְאַךְ יְהוָה לִפְנֵיהֶם: וְהָיָה בַּיּוֹם הַהוּא אֲבַקֵּשׁ לְהַשְׁמִיד אֶת־כָּל־הַגּוֹיִם הַבָּאִים עַל־
יְרוּשָׁלָם: וְשָׁפַכְתִּי עַל־בֵּית דָּוִיד וְעַל יוֹשֵׁב יְרוּשָׁלַם רוּחַ חֵן וְתַחֲנוּנִים וְהִבִּיטוּ אֵלַי אֵת אֲשֶׁר־דָּקָרוּ
וְסָפְדוּ עָלָיו כְּמִסְפֵּד עַל־הַיָּחִיד וְהָמֵר עָלָיו כְּהָמֵר עַל־הַבְּכוֹר: בַּיּוֹם הַהוּא יִגְדַּל הַמִּסְפֵּד בִּירוּשָׁלַם
כְּמִסְפַּד הֲדַד־רִמּוֹן בְּבִקְעַת מְגִדּוֹן: זכריה יב:ח-יא

OLD TESTAMENT SCRIPTURE TRANSLATION

"In that day the LORD will defend the inhabitants of Jerusalem, and the one who is feeble among them in that day will be like David, and the house of David *will be* like God, like the angel of the LORD before them. And it will come about in that day that I will set about to destroy all the nations that come against Jerusalem. And I will pour out on the house of David and on the inhabitants of Jerusalem, the Spirit of grace and of supplication, so that they will look on Me whom they have pierced; and they will mourn for Him, as one mourns for an only son, and they will weep bitterly over Him, like the bitter weeping over a first-born. In that day there will be great mourning in Jerusalem...." **Zechariah 12:8-11 NASB**

ANCIENT RABBINICAL COMMENTARY

"What is the cause of his mourning? In this Rabbi Dosa....said it was for Messiah, the son of Joseph, who is to be slain....If the cause will be the violent death of Messiah, the son of Joseph, one can understand that which is written, 'And they shall look to him whom they have pierced.' "[3]
Talmud Succah, fol. 52, col. 1

NEW TESTAMENT RECORDED 96 AD

"BEHOLD, HE IS COMING WITH THE CLOUDS, and every eye will see Him, even those who pierced Him; and all the tribes of the earth will mourn over Him. Even so. Amen." **Revelation 1:7 NASB**

MODERN RABBINICAL COMMENT/REFUTATION

"But I will pour upon the house of David, and upon the inhabitants of Jerusalem, the spirit of grace and of supplications: and they whom the *nations* were piercing shall look upon me, and shall mourn over it, as one mourneth for *his* only *son*, and shall be in bitterness over it, as one that is in bitterness for *his* firstborn."[4]
The Holy Scriptures: A Jewish Bible According to the Masoretic Text, © 1977

AUTHOR'S COMMENT—EVANGELICAL CHRISTIAN POSITION

As Jesus returns (to save Israel from a future Russian/Arab invasion between 2010-2030+), the Jews will realize that their leaders, along with Rome, pierced the one who was their Messiah. For nearly 2500 years, the Hebrew words of Zechariah's prophetic jewel have been preserved in their purity. However, as we examined various newer English translations, we found that an increasing number of them had begun to mutilate these ancient words of the Jewish prophet. For example, though it says in the original Hebrew (וְהִבִּיטוּ אֵלַי אֵת אֲשֶׁר־דָּקָרוּ): "...they [the people of Jerusalem] will look upon him, whom they have pierced," one modern translation now reads quite differently, as you can see above! In recent times, the rabbis have found it expedient to take it upon themselves to change and alter the words of Zechariah, apparently to ward off missionaries. Why has it become common practice in the twentieth century to arbitrarily change portions of Zechariah's prophecy? We believe this is happening due to the result of the latter day continuation of the Messiah Conspiracy! This conspiracy was orchestrated by the rabbis to prevent Jews from finding biblical reasons to believe in Messiah Jesus. Clearly, the comments in the Jewish 'Bible' quoted (which, in our opinion, is more of a refutation, since it is such a dishonest translation),[5] are deceptive. We can see this when we look at Rabbi Dosa's unbiased ancient interpretation recorded in the Talmud. We support the original Hebrew of Zechariah, the New Testament and Rabbi Dosa's rabbinic comment, over modern frauds perpetrated to deceive the innocent! Don't you?   **Philip Moore**

---

[3]Rev. B. Pick, Ph.D., *Old Testament Passages Messianically Applied by the Ancient Synagogue*, published in the compilation *Hebraica, A Quarterly Journal in the Interests of Semitic Study*, Vol. IV, p.248.
[4]*The Holy Scriptures: A Jewish Bible According to the Masoretic Text.* Tel Aviv, Israel: "Sinai" Publishing, © 1977, pp. 1331-1332.
[5]In our *opinion,* the translation is dishonest for the reasons we have stated.

"In the 20th century the Jews will return to Jerusalem...." "The manner I know not. Let time be the interpreter." Sir Isaac Newton, the greatest scientist of history, three centuries before the event. Newton also predicted the 2nd coming would occur in the 21st century.

This work contains long lost material that, until now, was forbidden reading, plus insights, from a biblical perspective, into the old and infamous prophecies of Nostradamus - a first!

The End of History—Messiah Conspiracy now available, and the soon-to-be-published abridged version of this comprehensive work, by Philip N. Moore.

"Wailing at Jerusalem's Western Wall"

This work contains incredible evidence of the greatest conspiracy of all time - The Messiah Conspiracy, whereby the rabbis of early times sought to cover up the prophe-cies of their own Bible indicating Jesus was their Messiah. The motives behind this are both fascinating and shocking! In the little known town of Yavne, a curse was devised to separate Jewish believers from non-believers, yet they persisted past our fourth century in notable numbers. Today, they are reemerging, amidst heavy-handed anger, in the rabbinical community. We cannot be neutral!

"As for the noserim [Hebrew for "Christians"] and the minim, may they perish immediately. Speedily may they be erased from the Book of Life, and may they not be reg-istered among the righteous."   *The Birkat ha Minim (a first century curse against Christians) ordered by Gamaliel II, circa 80 AD*

"To this day the sect exists in all the synagogues of the Jews, under the title of 'the Minim'; the Pharisees still curse it, and the people dub its adherents 'Nazarenes,' etc."
Jerome, fourth-fifth century

"...nation shall rise against nation...and there shall be...pestilences, [incurable diseases]...in divers places [AIDS now exists on all continents with no cure in sight]."
Jesus, Matthew 24:7 KJV. [ ] mine

Our work also includes: Einsten letters never before published • Saving of Jews by Christian Zionists during the Holocaust • Insight into the *unknown* Hebrew of the Gospels • The Rabin assassination - prophetic? • Evidence proving Creation over Evolution • Jesus' prophecy of massive end-time plagues, now being revealed in our late twentieth cen-tury through genetically engineered germ weapons • Much more on the Dead Sea scrolls, the approaching Apocalypse and what happens to us when we die!

Back Cover of *The End of History—Messiah Conspiracy*, by Philip N. Moore.

NIGHTMARE OF THE APOCALYPSE
ΑΠΟΚΑΛΥΨΙΣ

THE RABBI CONSPIRACY

Excerpts from
THE END OF HISTORY—MESSIAH CONSPIRACY
VOLUME II—ESSAYS

PHILIP N. MOORE
Researcher for Hal Lindsey

Hebrew prophecies regarding Jesus' (ישוע) two Messianic Comings—The Apocalypse and Israel are briefly covered and compared with rabbinic anti-missionary arguments. Germ warfare (for a 'peaceful depopulation'), petra and abortion are also discussed within a context to the End Times. A lecture by Rabbi Johnathan Cahn and a discourse on the stars by Dr. D. James Kennedy are included.

Nightmare of the Apocalypse The Rabbi Conspiracy, excerpts from
The End of History Messiah Conspiracy, Volume II Essays, by Philip N. Moore.

Israel and the Apocalypse of Newton, by Philip N. Moore.

"My hair stood on end as I read some of the things that Philip ... found."[1]

Hal Lindsey

ABOUT THE AUTHOR

Philip Nicholas Moore was born in Atlanta, Georgia in 1957. For many years, he studied Greek in Atlanta and then Hebrew at Ulpan Etzion in Jerusalem. He spent eight years in Israel researching ancient Jewish beliefs and dedicated several years to researching the theological manuscripts of Isaac Newton at the Hebrew University in Jerusalem.

Moore was a volunteer at the army base, Base Machena Natan, in Beersheba, Israel. He was also a volunteer on the Temple Mount excavation with archaeologists Elat and Binyamin Mazar, which yielded the discovery of the "first Temple gateway" in 1986.

For several years, Moore assisted in research for the well known Christian author Hal Lindsey. From 1988 to 1990, Moore was instrumental in the Hebrew dubbing and release of the film *Jesus* in Jerusalem.

Presently, Philip Moore, residing in Atlanta, Georgia, is completing research for his fourth book, *Israel and the Apocalypse of Newton.*

The author and Hal Lindsey examine high-priestly garments recently woven in Jerusalem by Orthodox Jews.

---

[1] Philip Moore, *The End of History: The Messiah Conspiracy* Vol. I, page xxi.

PHOTO AND ILLUSTRATION CREDITS

P. numbers following names represent the P. numbers in our book.

Bauminger, Arieh L. *The Righteous*, Third Edition. Jerusalem: Yad VaShem Martyrs and Heroes Remembrance Authority, P. 49 (bottom), used by permission.

Frankenberger, James: P. photo and illustration credits.

Hargrave, Alice Q., *Time* Magazine: P. 24 (bottom far right photo).

International Christian Embassy, Jerusalem: Pp. 46, 53, 54, 55, 56 (except for authors listing).

Jerusalem Post: P. 47.

Larkin, Clarence (The Clarence Larkin Estate): P. 28.

Moore, Philip N. Pp. table of contents, facing page to chapter 1 (bottom), 14, 22, 24 (top), 39, 43, 44, 48, 49 (top arrangement), 50, 51, 52, 54 (bottom left), 56 (bottom three right).

Moss, Gary, for *Time* magazine: P. 24 (bottom; second photo from right).

State of Israel Government Press Office, photography department: P. facing page to chapter 1 (top).

Strutt, William, "Peace": P. 31.

Syndics of Cambridge University Library, P. 19.

Taibbi, Cathy: P. 37.

Author with a few of the books he used in his research.